VOWEL SOUNDS

Symbol	Examples
a	**a**ct, b**a**t
ā	d**a**y, **a**ge
âr	**air**, d**are**
ä	f**a**ther, st**a**r
e	**e**dge, t**e**n
ē	sp**ee**d, mon**ey**
ə*	**a**go, syst**em**, eas**i**ly, c**o**mpete, foc**u**s
ēr	d**ear**, p**ier**
i	f**i**t, **i**s
ī	sk**y**, b**i**te
o	n**o**t, w**a**sp
ō	n**o**se, **o**ver
ô	l**a**w, **o**rder
oi	n**oi**se, enj**oy**
o͞o	tr**ue**, b**oo**t
oo	p**u**t, l**oo**k
y͞oo	c**u**te, **u**nited
ou	l**ou**d, c**ow**
u	f**u**n, **u**p
ûr	l**ear**n, **ur**ge, butt**er**, w**or**d

*This symbol, the *schwa*, represents the sound of unaccented vowels. It sounds like "uh."

CONSONANT SOUNDS

Symbol	Examples
b	**b**ack, ca**b**
ch	**ch**eap, ma**tch**, pic**t**ure
d	**d**oor, hea**d**
f	**f**an, lea**f**, **ph**one
g	**g**ive, do**g**
h	**h**er, be**h**ave
j	**j**ust, pa**g**e
k	**k**ing, ba**k**e, **c**ar
l	**l**eaf, ro**ll**
m	**m**y, ho**m**e
n	**n**ote, rai**n**
ng	si**ng**, ba**n**k
p	**p**ut, sto**p**
r	**r**ed, fa**r**
s	**s**ay, pa**ss**
sh	**sh**ip, pu**sh**
t	**t**o, le**t**
th	**th**in, wi**th**
TH	**TH**at, ba**TH**e
v	**v**alue, li**v**e
w	**w**ant, a**w**ay
y	**y**es, on**i**on
z	**z**oo, ma**z**e, ri**s**e
zh	plea**s**ure, vi**s**ion

Interactive Vocabulary
General Words

Interactive Vocabulary
General Words

Second Edition

Amy E. Olsen
Cuesta College

PEARSON
Longman

New York   San Francisco   Boston
London   Toronto   Sydney   Tokyo   Singapore   Madrid
Mexico City   Munich   Paris   Cape Town   Hong Kong   Montreal

Vice President and Editor-in-Chief: Joseph Terry
Senior Acquisitions Editor: Steven Rigolosi
Associate Editor: Barbara Santoro
Senior Marketing Manager: Melanie Craig
Senior Supplements Editor: Donna Campion
Production Manager: Donna DeBenedictis
Project Coordination, Text Design, and Electronic Page Makeup: Elm Street Publishing Services, Inc.
Cover Designer/Manager: John Callahan
Cover Art: **TL:** Getty Images Inc.–Stone Allstock; **TR:** Art Resource, N.Y.; **BL:** Getty Images Inc.–Stone Allstock;
   BR: Dorling Kindersley Media Library
Art Studios: Burmar; Gil Adams
Photo Researcher: Photosearch, Inc.
Manufacturing Manager: Lucy Hebard
Printer and Binder: Quebecor World Dubuque
Cover Printer: Coral Graphic Services, Inc.

Photo Credits: P. 11, David Young-Wolff/PhotoEdit; p. 23, Keith Brofsky/Getty Images, Inc.; p. 50 (top center),
Art Resource, New York; p. 50 (left bottom), Art Resource, New York; p. 50 (bottom right), Superstock, Inc.;
p. 53, © DiMaggio/Kalish/CORBIS; p. 56, Stephen Oliver/Dorling Kindersley Media Library; p. 58, Ryan McVay/
Getty Images, Inc.; p. 74 (top), © Ariel Skelley/CORBIS; p. 74 (bottom), Amwell/Getty Images, Inc.;
p. 92, Connie Coleman/Getty Images; p. 105, © Bob Daemmrich Photo, Inc.; p. 121, National Palace Museum,
Taipei, Taiwan; p. 129, Private Collection/Archives Charmet/Bridgeman Art Library; p. 131, Bettmann/CORBIS;
p. 116, Art Resource, NY

Library of Congress-in-Publication Data
Olsen, Amy E.
   Interactive vocabulary : general words / Amy E. Olsen.—2nd ed.
      p. cm.
   ISBN 0-321-10472-2 (alk. paper)
    1. Vocabulary—problems, exercises, etc. I Title.

PE1449.046 2003
428.1—dc21

                                                                        2003047468

Please visit our website at **http://www.ablongman.com/vocabulary**

ISBN 0-321-10472-2

1 2 3 4 5 6 7 8 9 10—QUD—06 05 04 03

Dedication

To my family, friends, students, and colleagues for the good times we have had reading and discussing books: feats aided by well-developed vocabularies!
   —*Amy E. Olsen*

Contents

PART I   Education

page 42

page 23

PART II   Hobbies

page 42

page 89

page 89

page 89

page 74

page 136

page 116

page 89

Preface

Because students benefit greatly from increased word power, the study of vocabulary should be enjoyable. Unfortunately, vocabulary workbooks often lose sight of this goal. To help make the study of vocabulary an exciting and enjoyable part of college study, I wrote *Interactive Vocabulary*. The second edition of this book keeps the elements that make learning vocabulary enjoyable and adds several new features in response to comments offered by instructors across the country who teach vocabulary and developmental reading courses.

The goal of this book—the first-level in a three-book interactive series—is to make the study of vocabulary fun through a variety of thematic readings, self-tests, and interactive exercises. As a casual glimpse through the book will indicate, these activities involve writing, personal experience, art, and many other formats. The goal of these activities is simple: to utilize individual learning styles to help students learn new words in a large number of contexts.

Underlying the text's strong visual appeal is a strong underlying philosophy: an essential part of learning vocabulary is repeated exposure to a word. *Interactive Vocabulary* provides eight exposures to each word in the text plus two more opportunities for exposure through the collaborative exercises and games in the Instructor's Manual.

ORGANIZATION OF THE BOOK

The text begins with a **Getting Started** chapter, which helps familiarize students with some of the tools of vocabulary acquisition. The "Parts of Speech" section within this chapter gives sample words and sentences for the eight parts of speech. "Using the Dictionary" dissects a sample dictionary entry and provides an exercise on using guide words.

Following the Getting Started section, the book is broken down into six parts—with each part focusing on a particular high-interest theme. **At the end of three themed parts is a chapter on word parts** that introduces prefixes, roots, and suffixes used throughout this book.

Three review chapters in the book focus on the preceding seven or eight chapters. They divide the words into different activity groups and test students' cumulative knowledge. The words appear in artistic, dramatic, written, test, and puzzle formats. These repeated and varied exposures increase the likelihood that the students will remember the words, not for one chapter or a test, but for life.

The book **concludes with an Analogies Appendix and a Flash Cards Appendix.** The Analogies Appendix explains how analogies work and provides sample analogies to help students work through the analogy self-tests contained in several chapters of the text. The Flash Cards Appendix teaches students how to create and use their own flash cards and provides flash card templates.

ORGANIZATION OF EACH CHAPTER

Interactive Vocabulary is an ideal text for both classroom work and self-study. Each five-page chapter includes the following:

- **Thematic Reading:** Because most vocabulary is acquired through reading, each chapter begins with a thematic reading that introduces ten vocabulary words in context. These readings come in a variety of formats including newspaper articles, journal entries, and interviews. The goal is to show that new words may be encountered anywhere. Rather than simply presenting a word list with definitions, the readings give students the opportunity to discover the meanings of these new words via context clues.

The themes for *Interactive Vocabulary* were chosen from areas most interesting to students of all ages. In choosing the words, I was guided by five factors: (1) relation to the chapter theme, (2) use in popular magazines such as *Newsweek*, (3) listings in such frequency guides as *The American Heritage Word Frequency Book* and *The Educator's Word Frequency Guide*, (4) occurrence in standardized tests such as the S.A.T., and (5) my own experiences teaching developmental reading and writing.

- **Predicting:** The second page of each chapter contains a Predicting activity that gives students the chance to figure out the meaning of each vocabulary word before looking at the definition. The Predicting section helps students learn the value of context clues in determining the meaning of a word. While the text does offer information on dictionary use, I strongly advocate the use of context clues as one of the most active methods of vocabulary development. (The answers to the Predicting sections appear in the back of the book.)

- **Word List:** Following the Predicting activity is a list of the words with a pronunciation guide, the part of speech, and a brief definition. I wrote these definitions with the idea of keeping them simple and nontechnical. Some vocabulary texts provide complicated dictionary definitions that include words students do not know; I've tried to make the definitions as friendly and as useful as possible.

- **Self-Tests:** Following the Word List are four Self-Tests in various formats. With these tests, students can monitor their comprehension. The tests include text and sentence completion, true/false situations, matching, and analogies. Some tests employ context-clue strategies such as synonyms, antonyms, and general meaning. Critical thinking skills are an important part of each test. (Answers to the self-tests appear in the Instructor's Manual.)

- **Interactive Exercise:** Following the Self-Tests is an Interactive Exercise that asks students to begin actively using the vocabulary words. The activity may include writing, answering questions, or making lists. The Interactive Exercises give students the chance to really think about the meanings of the words, and more importantly, they encourage students to begin using the words actively.

ADDITIONAL FEATURES

In addition to the features described above the text also includes the following:

- **Hints:** Some chapters include hints for developing vocabulary and study skills. The hints are brief and practical, and students will be able to make use of them in all of their college courses.

- **Pronunciation Key:** On the inside front cover is a pronunciation key to help students understand the pronunciation symbols used in this text. The inside front cover also offers some additional guidelines on pronunciation issues.

FEATURES NEW TO THIS EDITION

- **Refined Text Organization:** The book is now organized around six main themes, with three or four chapters relating to each theme. This thematic organization will help students connect vocabulary words that they have learned in one chapter with words learned in other chapters. Also, review chapters are now included after every seven, rather than every ten, chapters. Including review tests more frequently reinforces vocabulary words and their meanings more effectively.

- **Refined In-Chapter Organization:** The Interactive Exercises are now the last exercise provided in each chapter since these exercises are more likely to provide a greater benefit to students once they have completed all of the practice exercises in the chapter.

- **More Exercises:** Two additional practice exercises (titled Self-Tests) are now included in each chapter so that the length of each chapter has been increased to five, rather than four, pages. These extra exercises give students even further practice and opportunities to learn and remember each vocabulary word.
- **Added Content:** Where appropriate, the text now provides alternative meanings for those words that warrant this extra information.
- **Refined Answer Key:** The answer key provides the answers for Predicting exercises only; all other answers have been removed.
- **Updated Analogies Appendix:** The Analogies Appendix includes an introduction on how to solve analogy questions and also includes a more thorough explanation of analogies.
- **Updated CD-ROM:** The CD-ROM that accompanies *Interactive Vocabulary* has been updated to include more effective and relevant exercises.

THE TEACHING AND LEARNING PACKAGE

Each component of the teaching and learning package for *Interactive Vocabulary* has been carefully crafted to maximize the main text's value.

- **Instructor's Manual and Test Bank:** The Instructor's Manual and Test Bank, which is almost as long as the main text, includes options for additional classroom activities such as collaborative exercises and games. The Collaborative Exercises usually ask students to share their work on the Interactive Exercises in small groups or with the whole class. These exercises give students the opportunity to practice using the words with other people. Some of the games are individual; others are full-class activities. Some games have winners, and some are just for fun. The games may involve acting, drawing, or writing.

  The Test Bank, formatted for easy copying, includes three tests for each chapter as well as Mastery Tests to accompany the review chapters and full-book Mastery Tests that can be used as final exams. ISBN: 0-321-10475-7.
- *Interactive Vocabulary* **CD-ROM:** In the computer age many students enjoy learning via computers. Available with this text is the *Interactive Vocabulary* CD-ROM, which features additional exercises and tests that provide for even more interaction between the students and the words. The CD-ROM has an audio component that allows students to hear each chapter's thematic reading and the pronunciation of each word as often as they choose. Students are often reluctant to use the new words they learn because they aren't sure how to pronounce them. The pronunciation guides in each chapter do help to address this fear, but actually hearing the words spoken will give students greater confidence in using the words. Contact your Longman sales representative to order the student text packaged with the CD-ROM.

FOR ADDITIONAL READING AND REFERENCE

The Longman Basic Skills Package

In addition to the book-specific supplements discussed above, many other skills-based supplements are available for both instructors and students. All of these supplements are available either free or at greatly reduced prices.

- **The Dictionary Deal.** Two dictionaries can be shrink-wrapped with *Interactive Vocabulary* at a nominal fee. *The New American Webster Handy College Dictionary* is a paperback reference text with more than 100,000 entries. *Merriam Webster's Collegiate Dictionary,* tenth edition, is a hardback reference with a citation file of more than 14.5 million examples of English words drawn from actual use. For more information on how to shrinkwrap a dictionary with your text, please contact your Longman sales representative.
- **Longman Vocabulary Web site.** For additional vocabulary-related resources, visit our free vocabulary Web site at **http://www.ablongman.com/vocabulary.**

ACKNOWLEDGMENTS

I would like to thank the following reviewers for their helpful suggestions while the book took shape for both the first and second editions:

Kathy Beggs, Pikes Peak Community College
Diana Bosco, Suffolk County Community College
Janet Curtis, Fullerton College
Susan Deason, Aiken Technical College
Carol Dietrick, Miami-Dade Community College
Jean Gorgie, Santa Monica College
Miriam Kinard, Trident Technical College
Belinda Klau, Imperial Valley College
John M. Kopec, Boston University
Maggi Miller, Austin Community College
Donna L. Richardson-Hall
Kerry Segel, Saginaw Valley State University
Susan Sandmeier, Columbia Basin College
Mary E. Shortridge, Ashland Community College
Kathleen Sneddon, University of Nebraska, Lincoln
Shirley Wachtel, Middlesex Community College
Carolyn Wilkie, Indiana University of Pennsylvania

Additionally, I want to thank Steven Rigolosi, Senior Acquisitions Editor, Developmental English, at Longman. Steve was essential in creating this series of vocabulary texts that combine traditional and innovative approaches to vocabulary study. I want to thank Barbara Santoro, Associate Editor, English, at Longman, for her helpful comments for this second edition. I also want to express thanks to my students and the English Division at Cuesta College for their support. Finally, I want to express my gratitude to my family for thoughtfully listening to my ideas about this series.

I am proud to present the second edition of a book that truly does make learning vocabulary fun.

AMY E. OLSEN

ALSO AVAILABLE

Book 2 of the Interactive Vocabulary Series:
   Active Vocabulary: General and Academic Words by Amy E. Olsen and Patti C. Biley

Book 3 of the Interactive Vocabulary Series:
   Academic Vocabulary: Academic Words by Amy E. Olsen

To the Student

This book is designed to make learning vocabulary fun. You will increase the benefits of this book if you keep a few points in mind:

1. **Interact with the words.** Each chapter contains eight exposures to a word, and your instructor may introduce one or two additional activities. If you're careful in your reading and thorough in doing the activities for each chapter, learning the words will be fun and easy.

2. **Appreciate the importance of words.** The words for the readings were picked from magazines, newspapers, novels, and lists of words likely to appear on standardized tests (such as SAT, GRE). These are words you will encounter in the classroom and in everyday life. Learning these words will help you be a more informed citizen and make your academic life much richer. Even if you don't currently have an interest in one of the readings, keep an open mind: the words may appear in the article you read in tomorrow's newspaper or on an exam in one of next semester's classes. The readings also come in different formats as a reminder that you can learn new vocabulary anywhere, from an interview to a journal entry.

3. **Find your preferred learning style.** The book aims to provide exercises for all types of learners—visual, aural, and interpersonal. But only you can say which learning style works best for you. See which activities (drawings, acting, matching, completing stories) you like most, and replicate those activities when they aren't part of the chapter.

4. **Remember that learning is fun.** Don't make a chore out of learning new words, or any other new skill for that matter. If you enjoy what you're doing, you're more likely to welcome the information and to retain it.

Enjoy your journey through *Interactive Vocabulary!*

—AMY E. OLSEN

Interactive Vocabulary
General Words

Getting Started

PARTS OF SPEECH

There are eight parts of speech. A word's part of speech is based on how it is used in a sentence. Words can, therefore, be more than one part of speech. For an example, note how the word *punch* is used below.

nouns: (n.) name a person, place, or thing

EXAMPLES: Ms. Lopez, New Orleans, lamp, warmth

Ms. Lopez enjoyed her *trip* to *New Orleans* where she bought a beautiful *lamp*. The *warmth* of the *sun* filled *Claire* with *happiness*. I drank five *cups* of the orange *punch*.

pronouns: (pron.) take the place of a noun

EXAMPLES: I, me, you, she, he, it, her, we, they, my, which, that, anybody, everybody

Everybody liked the music at the party. *It* was the kind that made people want to dance. *They* bought a new car, *which* hurt their bank account.

verbs: (v.) express an action or state of being

EXAMPLES: enjoy, run, think, read, dance, am, is, are, was, were

Lily *read* an interesting book yesterday. I *am* tired. He *is* an excellent student. She *punched* the bully.

adjectives: (adj.) modify (describe or explain) a noun or pronoun

EXAMPLES: pretty, old, two, expensive, red, small

The *old* car was covered with *red* paint on *one* side. The *two* women met for lunch at an *expensive* restaurant. The *punch* bowl was empty soon after Uncle Al got to the party.

adverbs: (adv.) modify a verb, an adjective, or another adverb

EXAMPLES: very, shortly, first, too, soon, quickly, finally, furthermore, however

We will meet *shortly* after one o'clock. The *very* pretty dress sold *quickly*. I liked her; *however*, there was something strange about her.

prepositions: (prep.) placed before a noun or pronoun to make a phrase that relates to other parts of the sentence

EXAMPLES: after, around, at, before, by, from, in, into, of, off, on, through, to, up, with

He told me to be *at* his house *around* noon. You must go *through* all the steps to do the job.

conjunctions: (conj.) join words or other sentence elements and show a relationship between the connected items

EXAMPLES: and, but, or, nor, for, so, yet, after, although, because, if, since, than, when

I went to the movies, *and* I went to dinner on Tuesday. I will not go to the party this weekend *because* I have to study. I don't want to hear your reasons *or* excuses.

interjections: (interj.) show surprise or emotion

EXAMPLES: oh, hey, wow, ah, ouch

Oh, I forgot to do my homework! *Wow,* I got an A on the test!

USING THE DICTIONARY

There will be times when you need to use a dictionary for one of its many features; becoming familiar with dictionary **entries** will make using a dictionary more enjoyable. The words in a dictionary are arranged alphabetically. The words on a given page are signaled by **guide words** at the top of the page. If the word you are looking for comes alphabetically between these two words then your word is on that page.

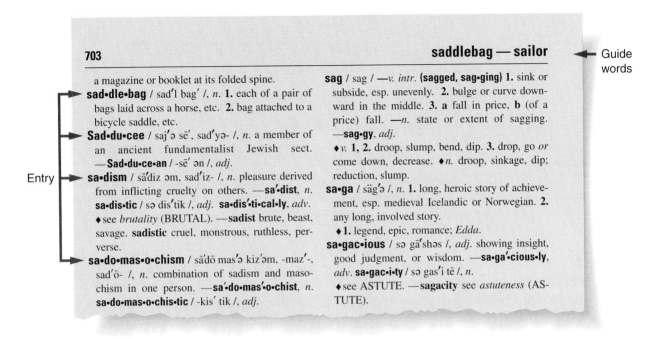

703   **saddlebag — sailor** ← Guide words

a magazine or booklet at its folded spine.
sad·dle·bag / sad′l bag′ /, *n.* **1.** each of a pair of bags laid across a horse, etc. **2.** bag attached to a bicycle saddle, etc.
Sad·du·cee / saj′ə sē′, sad′yə- /, *n.* a member of an ancient fundamentalist Jewish sect. —**Sad·du·ce·an** / -sē′ ən /, *adj.*
sa·dism / sā′diz əm, sad′iz- /, *n.* pleasure derived from inflicting cruelty on others. —**sa′·dist**, *n.* **sa·dis·tic** / sə dis′tik /, *adj.* **sa·dis′·ti·cal·ly**, *adv.* ♦ see *brutality* (BRUTAL). —**sadist** brute, beast, savage. **sadistic** cruel, monstrous, ruthless, perverse.
sa·do·mas·o·chism / sā′dō mas′ə kiz′əm, -maz′-, sad′ō- /, *n.* combination of sadism and masochism in one person. —**sa′·do·mas′·o·chist**, *n.* **sa·do·mas·o·chis·tic** / -kis′ tik /, *adj.*

sag / sag / —*v. intr.* (**sagged, sag·ging**) **1.** sink or subside, esp. unevenly. **2.** bulge or curve downward in the middle. **3. a** fall in price, **b** (of a price) fall. —*n.* state or extent of sagging. —**sag·gy**, *adj.*
♦*v.* **1, 2.** droop, slump, bend, dip. **3.** drop, go *or* come down, decrease. ♦*n.* droop, sinkage, dip; reduction, slump.
sa·ga / säg′ə /, *n.* **1.** long, heroic story of achievement, esp. medieval Icelandic or Norwegian. **2.** any long, involved story.
♦**1.** legend, epic, romance; *Edda.*
sa·ga·cious / sə gā′shəs /, *adj.* showing insight, good judgment, or wisdom. —**sa·ga′·cious·ly**, *adv.* **sa·gac·i·ty** / sə gas′i tē /, *n.*
♦see ASTUTE. —**sagacity** see *astuteness* (ASTUTE).

Entry

SOURCE: *The Oxford Desk Dictionary and Thesaurus, American Edition,* edited by Frank Abate, © 1996 by Oxford University Press, Inc. Used by permission of Oxford University Press, Inc.

Most dictionaries contain the following information in an entry:

- The **pronunciation**—symbols show how a word should be spoken, including how the word is divided into syllables and where the stress should be placed on a word. The Pronunciation Key for this book is located on the inside front cover. The key shows the symbols used to indicate the sound of a word. Every dictionary has a pronunciation method, and a pronunciation key or guide is usually found in the front pages, with a partial key at the bottom of each page. The differences in the pronunciation systems used by dictionaries are usually slight.
- The **part of speech**—usually abbreviated, such as *n.* for noun, *v.* for verb, and *adj.* for adjective. A key to these abbreviations and others is usually found in the front of the dictionary.
- The **definition**—usually the most common meaning is listed first followed by other meanings.
- An **example of the word in a sentence**—the sentence is usually in italics and follows each meaning.
- **Synonyms** and **antonyms**—*synonyms* are words with similar meanings, and *antonyms* are words that mean the opposite. (You should also consider owning a **thesaurus**, a book that lists synonyms and antonyms.)
- The **etymology**—the history of a word, usually including the language(s) it came from.
- The **spelling of different forms** of the word—these forms may include unusual plurals and verb tenses (especially irregular forms).

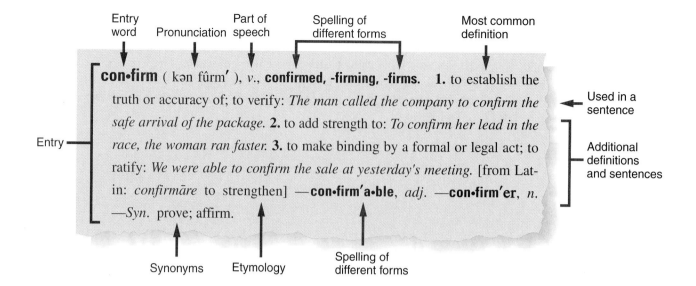

Entry word   Pronunciation   Part of speech   Spelling of different forms   Most common definition

Entry

con•firm (kən fûrm′), v., **confirmed, -firming, -firms.** **1.** to establish the truth or accuracy of; to verify: *The man called the company to confirm the safe arrival of the package.* **2.** to add strength to: *To confirm her lead in the race, the woman ran faster.* **3.** to make binding by a formal or legal act; to ratify: *We were able to confirm the sale at yesterday's meeting.* [from Latin: *confirmāre* to strengthen] —**con•firm′a•ble**, *adj.* —**con•firm′er**, *n.* —*Syn.* prove; affirm.

Used in a sentence

Additional definitions and sentences

Synonyms   Etymology   Spelling of different forms

When choosing a dictionary, take the time to look at different dictionaries and see what appeals to you. Dictionaries come in several sizes and are made for different purposes. First read some of the entries and see if the definitions make sense to you. See which of the features above are used in the dictionary. Is it important to you to be able to study the etymology of a word? Would you like sample sentences? Some dictionaries have illustrations in the margins. Decide if that is a feature you would use. Check to see if the print is large enough for you to read easily.

Decide on how you will use this dictionary. Do you want a paperback dictionary to put in your backpack? Or is this going to be the dictionary for your desk and a large hardback version would be the better choice? Several disciplines have specialized dictionaries with meanings that apply to those fields, such as law or medicine. There are also bilingual dictionaries, such as French/English or Spanish/English that can be helpful for school or travel. Take time in picking out your dictionary because a good dictionary will be a companion for years to come. A few dictionaries to consider are *Webster's College Dictionary, The American Heritage Dictionary, The Random House College Dictionary,* and *The Oxford Dictionary.*

In general, when you are reading try to use context clues, the words around the word you don't know, to first figure out the meaning of a word, but if you are still in doubt don't hesitate to refer to a dictionary for the exact definition. Don't forget that dictionaries also contain more than definitions and are an essential reference source for any student.

HINT

You can understand the meaning of a word without knowing how to pronounce it correctly; however, sometimes if you sound out a new word using phonics, you will realize you've heard the word before, which may help you to understand its meaning.

Using Guide Words

Use the sample guide words to determine on which page each of the ten words will be found. Write the page number next to the entry word.

Page	Guide Words
157	bone/boo
159	boot/born
435	endemic/endorse
654	humanist/humongous
655	humor/hunter
975	pamphlet/pandemonium
976	pander/pant
1480	velvet/venom

EXAMPLE: _654_ humdinger

_____ 1. pane

_____ 2. panda

_____ 3. bonnet

_____ 4. vendor

_____ 5. ending

_____ 6. Hungarian

_____ 7. borax

_____ 8. pandowdy

_____ 9. humid

_____ 10. humble

Entry Identification

Label the parts of the following entry:

a•ble (ā′ bəl) *adj.* **a•bler, a•blest.** 1. having the necessary power, skill, or qualifications to do something: *She was able to read music.*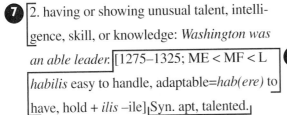

2. having or showing unusual talent, intelligence, skill, or knowledge: *Washington was an able leader.* [1275–1325; ME < MF < L  *habilis* easy to handle, adaptable=*hab(ere)* to have, hold + *ilis* –ile] Syn. apt, talented.

1. _____

2. _____

3. _____

4. _____

5. _____

6. _____

7. _____

8. _____

9. _____

1

Vocabulary Basics

Cafeteria Views

Predicting

Circle the definition that best fits each vocabulary word. If you have difficulty, return to the reading on page 6, and underline any context clues you find. After you've made your predictions, check your answers against the Word List below. Place a checkmark in the boxes next to the words whose definitions you missed. These are the words you'll want to study closely.

NOTE: You may want to cover the Word List below with a piece of paper so you don't accidentally see the definitions as you do the Predicting exercise.

☐ 1. **antonym** (bubble 2)
   a. words that rhyme
   b. word with a similar meaning
   c. word that means the opposite

☐ 2. **predict** (bubble 4)
   a. to worry
   b. to tell in advance
   c. to get money in advance

☐ 3. **synonym** (bubble 6)
   a. a place of worship
   b. word with a similar meaning
   c. word that means the opposite

☐ 4. **theme** (bubble 9)
   a. a topic
   b. a disease
   c. something used in healing

☐ 5. **analogy** (bubble 10)
   a. a comparison
   b. a type of ghost
   c. a way of speaking

☐ 6. **interactive** (bubble 12)
   a. revolving around the solar system
   b. moving something around in the room
   c. requiring active thought and communication

☐ 7. **context clues** (bubble 14)
   a. a mystery
   b. words around another word that give hints about its meaning
   c. a game where the winner gets a prize

☐ 8. **phonics** (bubble 16)
   a. using the telephone
   b. playing the telephone game
   c. sounding out a word

☐ 9. **collaborative** (bubble 17)
   a. collecting money at church
   b. eating with others
   c. working together

☐ 10. **diligent** (bubble 18)
   a. working in a careful way
   b. working in a careless way
   c. working during summer

Word List

analogy [ə nal′ ə jē]	*n.* a comparison; likeness	**phonics** [fon′ iks]	*n.* a reading method in which letters are associated with their sounds or pronunciation
antonym [an′ tə nim]	*n.* word that means the opposite		
collaborative [kə lab′ ûr ə tiv′]	*adj.* working together; working with other people	**predict** [pri dikt′]	*v.* to tell in advance
context clues [kon′ tekst klooz′]	*n.* words around another word that give hints about its meaning	**synonym** [sin′ ə nim]	*n.* word with a similar meaning
diligent [dil′ ə jənt]	*adj.* steady and energetic; careful		
interactive [in′ tûr ak′ tiv]	*adj.* requiring active thought and communication; making connections	**theme** [thēm]	*n.* a specific or focused subject or topic

Self-Tests

1 Match each term with its definition.

SET ONE

_____ 1. diligent

_____ 2. phonics

_____ 3. analogy

_____ 4. collaborative

_____ 5. context clues

a. words around another word that hint at its meaning

b. a comparison

c. steady and energetic

d. a reading method associating sounds with words

e. working together

SET TWO

_____ 6. theme

_____ 7. predict

_____ 8. interactive

_____ 9. antonym

_____ 10. synonym

f. word with a similar meaning

g. making connections

h. word that means the opposite

i. to tell in advance

j. a specific topic

2 Pick the best word from the list below to complete the sentence. Use each word once.

Vocabulary List

synonym	interactive	theme	collaborative	antonyms
diligent	analogy	phonics	predict	context clues

1. I went to see a fortune-teller to hear her _____ whether I would be rich someday.

2. The _____ for our first paper in English class was technology.

3. I listened to ten _____ tapes in the reading lab to improve my pronunciation.

4. The student made an interesting _____ between writing a paper and riding a bike.

5. The woman wanted to become an executive in the company, so she was _____ at her job.

6. Making a movie is a _____ project because it involves writers, actors, technicians, and the director to put it together.

7. When I am reading and come across a word I don't know, I look for _____ to help me figure out the meaning.

8. Using a computer can be _____ because some programs tell you if your answer is right or wrong, and then you can think about your choices and make changes.

9. When I want to stop repeating the same word in a paper, but I need another word with the same meaning, I look in a thesaurus to find a _____.

10. *Stubborn* and *flexible* are important _____ to learn. I discovered the difference between the two when my friends told me to stop being stubborn and start being more flexible or they wouldn't see me anymore.

3 Circle the word that correctly completes each sentence.

1. By using (antonyms, phonics) I can usually correctly pronounce new words.

2. I didn't like (diligent, collaborative) projects until I met my boyfriend while working on a history class assignment with him.

3. I tried to (predict, interactive) what my biology teacher would ask on the exam, and I did a good job—I knew all but two of the questions.

4. I have found that using (phonics, synonyms) has made my writing more interesting to read.

5. Now that I am aware of (phonics, context clues) I can figure out the meaning of unknown words much easier.

6. I was so (diligent, collaborative) about doing my homework on Friday that I was able to go to the party on Saturday.

7. My sister made the (analogy, phonics) that her vacation was like spending a week in a life raft. After hearing about all the problems she had, I think she was right.

8. I like my Spanish class because the professor makes it (diligent, interactive); we participate in some way everyday.

9. The (antonym, theme) for my first speech is how to improve the college.

10. My friend described the cake as "tasty," but I can think of several (antonyms, analogies) that would fit it better: horrid, rotten, gross.

4 Answer each question by writing the vocabulary word on the line next to the example it best fits. Use each word once.

1. Cold, freezing, and chilly are what type of words for hot? _____

2. Keri proofreads her papers six times. What kind of student is she? _____

3. After he looks at the clouds, Matt says it is going to rain. What is he doing? _____

4. Tony announces that the topic of the meeting is "how to raise funds for a club trip." What is he providing for the meeting? _____

5. June says, "Life is one big tea party." What kind of comparison has she made? _____

6. Warm, boiling, and sweltering are what type of words for hot? _____

7. Milt looks up "chrome" in the dictionary and finds the pronunciation krōm. What is he using to help him pronounce the word? _____

8. When a brother and sister help each other pick up their toys, they are being? _____

9. Katy connects her history lecture to a short story she read in English. What type of learning is she using? _____

10. Dan says, "I am famished. I haven't eaten anything since yesterday." If you use the sentence "I haven't eaten anything since yesterday" to figure out the meaning of famished, what have you benefited from? _____

Vocabulary List

analogy

collaborative

diligent

phonics

synonyms

interactive

predicting

antonyms

theme

context clues

Interactive Exercise

Write a note to a classmate about your attitude toward studying vocabulary words. Use at least five of the vocabulary words introduced in this chapter. Use the space below to draft your note.

Dear _____ ,

_____

_____

_____

_____

_____

_____

_____

_____

Sincerely,

_____

College Life

An Exciting Adventure

Juanita was the first person in her family to go to college. Her family had moved to California from Mexico when she was two years old. She was excited but also nervous about entering college. She knew that getting an education would **empower** her to get a better job. With hope and fear, she kissed her parents and headed off to the college for **orientation**. 5

10

At the orientation workshop a **counselor** told her and the other students how to select classes, what tests they needed to take, and what services the college provided to help them succeed. Juanita had to take **assessment** tests in English and math to see what level class she should start at. After the general meeting, Juanita met with a counselor. 15

"Juanita, do you know what you want to **major** in? What are your interests?" asked Ms. Maxwell.

"I'm not sure. I do like math and art." 20

"We have excellent **faculty** who teach in both areas. You should take classes in both subjects and get to know the professors; they can help you make up your mind. You don't have to **declare** your major right away. You can wait until you have a clear idea of what you want to study before you formally tell the college. I would also suggest taking an **aptitude** test to see what areas you may have special talents in." 25

"Thank you for talking with me Ms. Maxwell. I feel I can better **cope** with college after coming to today's orientation."

"You have made a **commitment** to your future by coming today, and I am sure you will be able to deal with the pressures of college. But if you ever need any assistance don't hesitate to come to this office for help." 30

Juanita left the college excited and no longer nervous about her new environment.

Predicting

Circle the definition that best fits each vocabulary word. If you have difficulty, return to the reading on page 11, and underline any context clues you find. After you've made your predictions, check your answers against the Word List below. Place a checkmark in the boxes next to the words whose definitions you missed. These are the words you'll want to study closely.

NOTE: You may want to cover the Word List below with a piece of paper so you don't accidentally see the definitions as you do the Predicting exercise.

☐ 1. **empower** (line 8)
  a. to persuade
  b. to limit
  c. to permit

☐ 2. **orientation** (line 12)
  a. technical training
  b. study skills
  c. program to help people adjust

☐ 3. **counselor** (line 13)
  a. gym teacher
  b. registrar
  c. advisor

☐ 4. **assessment** (line 15)
  a. testing
  b. acceptance
  c. assignment

☐ 5. **major** (line 18)
  a. the main area of study
  b. income
  c. a career

☐ 6. **faculty** (line 21)
  a. buildings
  b. facilities
  c. teachers

☐ 7. **declare** (line 23)
  a. to announce
  b. to hide
  c. to capture

☐ 8. **aptitude** (line 25)
  a. funding
  b. a strange feeling
  c. talent

☐ 9. **cope** (line 26)
  a. to survive
  b. to give in
  c. to practice

☐ 10. **commitment** (line 28)
  a. a promise
  b. a lie
  c. a group of people

Word List

aptitude
[ap′ tə to͞od′]
n. 1. talent
2. quickness in learning; intelligence

assessment
[ə ses′ mənt]
n. testing; evaluation

commitment
[kə mit′ mənt]
n. a promise

cope
[kōp]
v. to survive; to handle

counselor
[koun′ sə lûr]
n. advisor; person who counsels

declare
[di klâr′]
v. to announce formally; strongly assert

empower
[em pou′ ər, im-]
v. to authorize; to enable; to permit

faculty
[fak′ əl tē]
n. teachers at a school, college, or university

major
[mā′ jûr]
n. the principal area of study chosen by a student in college
adj. greater in importance; serious

orientation
[ôr′ ē ən tā′ shən]
n. program intended to help people adapt to a new environment

Self-Tests

1 Write the letter of the vocabulary word next to its definition.

_____ 1. instructors   a. declare

_____ 2. to handle   b. counselor

_____ 3. a promise   c. major

_____ 4. talent   d. assessment

_____ 5. to permit   e. faculty

_____ 6. main area of study f. aptitude

_____ 7. to announce   g. orientation

_____ 8. person who gives advice h. cope

_____ 9. program to help students adapt i. commitment

_____ 10. testing   j. empower

2 Juanita is taking classes in France for a year. Fill in the blanks of her letter to her parents with the appropriate vocabulary word. Use each word once.

Vocabulary List

cope	assessment	counselor	faculty	major
orientation	declare	empowered	aptitude	commitment

Dear Mom and Dad,

The semester is going well. I am really happy with my (1) _____; International Business suits me well. We had an excellent (2) _____ to the program during the first week. They told us about our classes and took us on a city tour of Paris to become familiar with the city. The (3) _____ test I took before I came over put me in the right level of French. I understand most of what the professor says. The (4) _____ here are great. They are friendly and helpful with the course work and with understanding a different culture. I am taking a cooking class for fun and have found I have quite the (5) _____ for making crepes. I can't wait to cook for you when I get home. At first it was a little hard to (6) _____ with the differences in cultures, especially hearing French all day, but now it is not that hard. Thank you for your (7) _____ to my education. Your help has made this trip possible. Next week I go to the (8) _____ to get advice on what classes to take next semester. This experience has (9) _____ me to go on to graduate school. I want to get a Master's in Business Administration next. You might think that is a lot to (10) _____ after eight weeks in France, but I know I can do it. I hope all is well at home. I will write more later.

Love,

Juanita

3 Put a T for true or F for false next to each statement.

_____ 1. Learning to read will not empower a person to do better in school.

_____ 2. It can be hard to cope with planning a wedding.

_____ 3. A candidate needs to declare that he or she is running for office.

_____ 4. The faculty at most colleges usually have no more than a high school education.

_____ 5. A company might hold an orientation for new employees.

_____ 6. A counselor's main job is to teach swimming.

_____ 7. If Monica has an aptitude for singing, she is likely to be a good singer.

_____ 8. If you make a commitment to feeding the homeless on Saturdays, you don't have to show up regularly.

_____ 9. Balancing work, school, and family can be a major problem.

_____ 10. After a hurricane, various government and insurance agencies will make an assessment of the damages.

4 The following are comments heard around a college campus. Finish each sentence using the vocabulary words below. Use each word once.

SET ONE

Vocabulary List				
declare	faculty	cope	orientation	aptitude

1. "Thanks to my friend Joe's help, I was able to _____ with geometry."

2. "I have decided to _____ my major as art. I am going to fill out the paper work tomorrow."

3. "I just discovered that I have a(n) _____ for tap dancing!"

4. "I appreciate the _____ on this campus; two of my favorite professors are Remsburg and Ramsey."

5. "I learned about tutoring services at the _____ meeting I came to the week before classes began."

SET TWO

Vocabulary List				
counselor	empower	major	assessment	commitment

6. "I will be at the study session tonight. When I make a(n) _____, I stick to it."

7. "I have to go to the _____ office to sign up for a writing test. I want to be placed in the right level of English next semester."

8. "Mr. Diaz is an excellent _____; he told me all about a program the college offers for students who are having problems studying."

9. "I am not sure if I want my _____ to be law or drama."

10. "Next week I become editor of the college newspaper, which will _____ me to make the changes the paper needs."

Interactive Exercise

Draw a simple map of your school or college campus. Label the map with at least five vocabulary words showing where you go to do activities at your school. For example, show where you go for *orientation,* where *faculty* offices are located, and where students can visit their *counselors.* You can be imaginative with some of the labels: where you go if you have an *aptitude* for music, where you go to *cope* with writing problems.

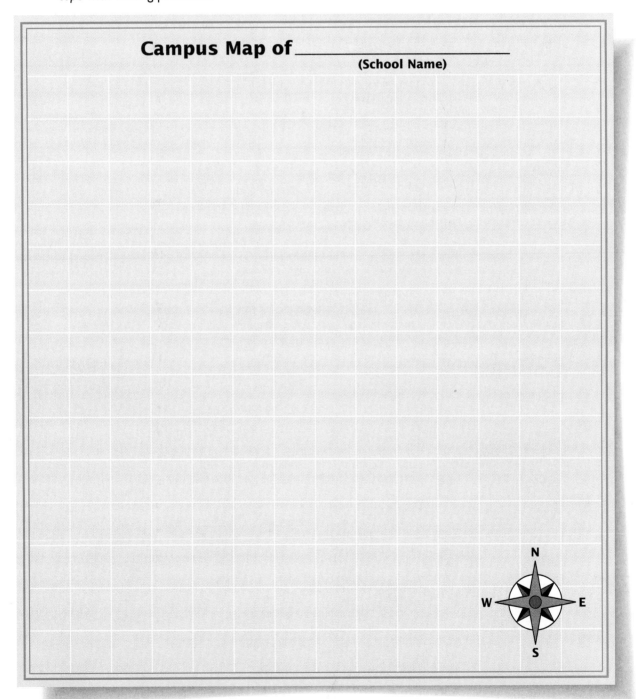

Campus Map of _____
(School Name)

3 Time Management

Elizabeth's Time Management System

① **Announcer:** This is KHBG Talk Radio, the voice of the campus.

② **Ralph:** Good afternoon, one and all. I'm Ralph Howard, your host. Tonight we have a special program lined up for you. Our guest is Elizabeth Downs, author of the best-selling book, *Elizabeth's Time **Management** System*. Elizabeth, welcome to the show.

③ **Elizabeth:** Thank you, Ralph. It's a pleasure to be here.

④ **Ralph:** Before we open up the phone lines to take questions from our listeners, could you please tell us why you decided to write this book?

⑤ **Elizabeth:** That's an easy one. I was a **disorganized** person who never seemed to **accomplish** anything. In spite of my plans, I always **procrastinated**.

⑥ **Ralph:** In other words, you waited to do things you had to do until the last minute.

⑦ **Elizabeth:** That's right. But that was before I learned how to **prioritize**. Now I do things in the order of their importance. The key is keeping a master list of things that need to get done.

⑧ **Ralph:** We have a caller on the line now. Lisa, are you there?

⑨ **Lisa:** Yes. I have a question for Elizabeth. I haven't read your book yet, and I need help. I'm a **frazzled** student, mother, and wife. I'm tired and frustrated because I'm constantly doing things for my husband and my kids, so I rarely get the cleaning done and don't have enough time to study.

⑩ **Elizabeth:** You are going to have to take the **initiative** and get your family more involved in the housework. Make a list of all the cleaning jobs in your home. Schedule a day for each of them and a job for each person to do. The key to this approach is to not give up. If someone misses a day, remind the person, but continue the weekly schedule. Eventually everyone will participate, and the work will get done, and you won't be so exhausted.

⑪ **Lisa:** Oh, thank you!

⑫ **Ralph:** Jerry, are you there?

⑬ **Jerry:** Yes, thank you. Elizabeth, I hope you can help me. I'm always late. No matter how early I start something, I never meet my deadlines. I'm just not as **efficient** as I want to be.

⑭ **Elizabeth:** Do you have a weekly planner? No? Well, get one. Keep a record of all your appointments and assignments. Once a week sit down and list everything that you need to do. Estimate how much time each **task** will take. Then, decide when you are going to do it. Write it on the planner. Check the planner throughout the week, and when the time comes to do the job you will be prepared because you have **allotted** the time for it. You'll be more efficient and productive than ever.

Predicting

Circle the definition that best fits each vocabulary word. If you have difficulty, return to the reading on page 16, and underline any context clues you find. After you've made your predictions, check your answers against the Word List below. Place a checkmark in the boxes next to the words whose definitions you missed. These are the words you'll want to study closely.

NOTE: You may want to cover the Word List below with a piece of paper so you don't accidentally see the definitions as you do the Predicting exercise.

❑ 1. **management** (bubble 2)
    a. decision
    b. employment
    c. control

❑ 2. **disorganized** (bubble 5)
    a. not in order
    b. dirty
    c. official

❑ 3. **accomplish** (bubble 5)
    a. to accept
    b. to complete
    c. to regret

❑ 4. **procrastinate** (bubble 5)
    a. to pass
    b. to postpone
    c. to increase

❑ 5. **prioritize** (bubble 7)
    a. to put away
    b. to do carefully
    c. to place in order of importance

❑ 6. **frazzled** (bubble 9)
    a. tired
    b. happy
    c. bored

❑ 7. **initiative** (bubble 10)
    a. false step
    b. first step
    c. last step

❑ 8. **efficient** (bubble 13)
    a. admirable
    b. orderly
    c. with effort

❑ 9. **task** (bubble 14)
    a. order
    b. job
    c. tale

❑ 10. **allotted** (bubble 14)
    a. assigned
    b. missed
    c. followed

Word List

accomplish [ə käm′ plish]	*v.* to complete; to carry out		**initiative** [i nish′ ē ə tiv]	*n.* the first step; the ability to start a plan
allot [ə lot′]	*v.* to give; to assign		**management** [man′ ij mənt]	*n.* 1. the ability to control something 2. the people who direct a business
disorganized [dis ôr′ gə nīzd′]	*adj.* not having order; confused; messy		**prioritize** [prī ôr′ ə tīz′]	*v.* to place in order of importance
efficient [ē fish′ ənt, i fish′ ənt]	*adj.* orderly; effective; well-organized		**procrastinate** [pro kras′ tə nāt′]	*v.* to postpone; to put off
frazzled [fraz′ əld]	*adj.* tired; exhausted		**task** [task]	*n.* an assignment; a job; a chore

Self-Tests

Match the description with one of the vocabulary words below. Context clues are underlined to help you make the connections. Use each word once.

1. _____ I will give myself two hours to write a rough draft of my paper; however, I will assign a lot more time to revising it.

2. _____ Dexter not only earned a bachelor's degree with high honors, but he was also able to complete his degree in three years.

3. _____ Jay puts off doing anything until the last minute.

4. _____ Ali took the first step and held a meeting to organize a food drive; we appreciated her getting us started.

5. _____ It's more important to study for my test than watch television tonight.

6. _____ Isis is so organized that she never forgets any birthdays or anniversaries.

7. _____ I feel tired and stressed.

8. _____ One of the chores I have to do today is wash the clothes.

9. _____ Patricia is so confused that she forgets appointments and loses things.

10. _____ It has taken a while, but I finally feel that I have the ability to control my finances.

Vocabulary List

initiative

efficient

prioritize

allot

disorganized

task

frazzled

procrastinate

management

accomplish

2 For each set, complete the analogies. See the Analogies Appendix on page 143 for instructions and practice.

SET ONE

1. lose : disorganized :: _____
2. faculty : student :: _____
3. day : night :: _____
4. page : notebook :: _____
5. pencil : write :: _____

a. task : project
b. find : efficient
c. planner : prioritize
d. fail : accomplish
e. management : secretary

SET TWO

6. wasteful : careful :: _____
7. run : a marathon :: _____
8. gamble : money :: _____
9. drink : thirst :: _____
10. job: work :: _____

f. disorganized : confused
g. procrastinate : time
h. allot : forty dollars to spend on shoes
i. laziness : initiative
j. rest : frazzled

18 PART I EDUCATION

3 Finish the want ads from the business section. Use each word once.

Help Wanted

1. Looking for a(n) _____ secretary. You must be able to _____ projects. You must be able to work on several _____ at one time. _____ need not apply—meeting deadlines is essential to our business. Send your resume to Human Resources, 115 Industrial Rd., Suite B, Hillsdale, 92111.

Help Wanted

2. If you aren't easily _____, apply to be the head of our Complaints Department. Move into _____ and take control of your career. If you know how to carefully _____ your time, call (555) 364-2100 today.

Help Wanted

3. _____ office needs help! If you have the _____ to straighten our files and books, we want you. We need someone to _____ our orders, and get this small operation back on track. Call now (555) 460-3221.

CAREER OPPORTUNITIES

4 Circle the correct meaning of each vocabulary word.

1. **accomplish:**	do	failure
2. **disorganized:**	confused	neat
3. **efficient:**	messy	orderly
4. **frazzled:**	tired	rested
5. **initiative:**	first step	do nothing
6. **allot:**	assign	remove
7. **management:**	unsure	control
8. **prioritize:**	random	order of importance
9. **procrastinate:**	put off	get started
10. **task:**	game	job

Interactive Exercise

Write your answers in one or two sentences. Use a vocabulary word in each answer. Your plan is to move into *management*. The company will not consider you until you have answered its questionnaire.

HOW ORGANIZED ARE YOU?

1. Do you usually *accomplish* your *tasks* or goals? Why or why not?

   _____

   _____

2. Which word describes you the most—*efficient, disorganized* or *frazzled*? Explain.

   _____

   _____

3. Describe a situation when you *procrastinated*.

   _____

   _____

4. Describe a situation where you took the *initiative*.

   _____

   _____

5. Do you use a planner to help you *allot* your time, or *prioritize* your duties? Explain why or why not.

   _____

   _____

HINT

A Word about Context Clues

When you encounter a word whose meaning you don't know, keep reading the passage looking for clues to help you decipher the meaning. These clues might be in the same sentence as the unknown word or in a sentence that comes before or after the word. Look for these types of clues in the passage:

Synonyms—words that have a similar meaning to the unknown word
Antonyms—words that mean the opposite of the unknown word
Examples—a list of items that explain the unknown word
General meaning—the meaning of the sentence or passage as a whole that could clarify the meaning of the unknown word

You will not find a context clue every time you encounter a word you don't know, but being aware of context clues will help you determine the meaning of many new words and make reading more enjoyable.

4 Word Parts I

Look for words with these **prefixes**, **roots**, and/or **suffixes** as you work through this book. You may have already seen some of them, and you will see others in later chapters. Learning basic word parts can help you figure out the meanings of unfamiliar words.

prefix: a word part added to the beginning of a word that changes the meaning of the root
root: a word's basic part with its essential meaning
suffix: a word part added to the end of a word; indicates the part of speech

WORD PART	MEANING	EXAMPLES AND DEFINITIONS
Prefixes		
dis-	away from, not	*disorganized:* not organized *disappear:* move away from sight
inter-	between, among	*interactive:* making connections between things *international:* between nations or countries
pre-	before	*predict:* to tell in advance *preview:* to see before
Roots		
-chron-	time	*chronological:* following time order *chronic:* all the time
-dic-, -dict-	to say, to tell, to use words	*predict:* to tell in advance *dictation:* the process of saying or reading aloud to be recorded or written by someone else
-man-, -manu-	hand	*manuscript:* a handwritten document *manually:* done by hand
-ten-	to stretch	*intention:* a plan (to stretch toward) *intense:* to an extreme degree (stretched tight)
Suffixes		
-ment (makes a noun)	action, state of being	*assessment:* state of assessing or measuring *merriment:* the state of being merry
-or, -er (makes a noun)	one who	*counselor:* a person who counsels or gives advice *baker:* a person who bakes
-tion, -ation (makes a noun)	condition, act of	*opposition:* the act of opposing or being in conflict *action:* condition of being active or doing

Self-Tests

Read each definition and choose the appropriate word from the list below. Use each word once. The meaning of the word part is underlined to help you make the connection. Refer to the Word Part list on page 21 if you need help.

Vocabulary List

enchantment	manage	extend	predict	chronological
discourage	intersperse	philosopher	imitation	dictionary

1. to say before   _____

2. to stretch out   _____

3. to distribute between things   _____

4. to be able to handle   _____

5. relating to time order   _____

6. a person who is wise   _____

7. the state of being charmed   _____

8. a book on how to use words   _____

9. condition of being false   _____

10. to take away one's hope   _____

Finish the sentences with the meaning of each word part from the list below. Use each meaning once. The word part is underlined to help you make the connection.

Vocabulary List

not	hand	person who	to stretch	before
tells	between	state of being	act of	time

1. When you go to a preview of a movie, you see it _____ other people do.

2. The Olympics is an international event. This means it is held _____ different countries.

3. To have chronic pain means to have pain all the _____ or constantly.

4. An actor is a _____ acts.

5. If someone is feeling merriment, he or she is in the _____ merry.

6. When giving a verdict, the jury _____ the decision it has made.

7. To set up the tent we had _____ it over the poles.

8. If you do something manually, you do it by _____.

9. If you dislike someone, you do _____ like him or her.

10. Graduation is the _____ finishing school.

3 Finish the story using the word parts below. Use each word part once. Your knowledge of word parts, as well as the context clues, will help you create the correct words. If you do not understand the meaning of a word you have made, check the dictionary for the definition or to see whether the word exists.

Word Parts

ation	pre	tend	inter	er
dic	man	chron	dis	ment

The Job

June was worried about her _____view. She really needed a job. She sat in the waiting room thinking about her skills. She knew how to be-have in a professional manner. She could speak to people on the telephone and make them feel like the company cared about them. She could also _____tate well—she had no problem telling other people what to do. She knew she would be a good office _____ager.

As she waited in the office, she looked at the other applicants. She could tell one man was very nervous although he was trying to pre_____ he wasn't. June sympathized with him be-cause she felt the same way. June went to sit next to him. She told him that she also _____liked looking for a job. Milt told her that this was not a situ_____ he enjoyed. There was too much to _____pare for. June asked Milt what time it was. She suggested they syn_____ize their watches, so they could meet at the coffee shop at the same time after the interviews. Milt thought that was a great idea as it would ease his resent_____ of having to go through the interview process. They agreed that it was frustrating to be interviewed. They started to talk when the inter-view_____ called June's name.

4 Pick the best definition for each underlined word using your knowledge of word parts. Circle the word part in each of the underlined words.

a. likely to act a certain way

b. state of being satisfied

c. not at the proper time

d. came between

e. to move away from

f. one who translates

g. planned beforehand

h. to say the opposite

i. way of handling things

j. act of expressing joy

_____ 1. The police knew the murder had been <u>premeditated</u> when they found the receipt for the poison dated a week ago.

_____ 2. Her <u>manner</u> was so friendly that I felt relaxed right away at the party.

_____ 3. It was easy to find the <u>anachronism</u> in the picture of the medieval castle: the microwave.

_____ 4. The police told the crowd to <u>disperse</u> because the rally was over.

_____ 5. My boyfriend always <u>contradicts</u> me. Why can't he ever agree with me?

_____ 6. My sister has a <u>tendency</u> to exaggerate; I never know when to believe her.

_____ 7. Mother <u>intervened</u> when the argument between my brother and me got so serious we were about to hit each other.

_____ 8. The <u>translator</u> had a hard job when everyone spoke at the same time.

_____ 9. I appreciated the <u>congratulation</u> cards from my friends when I passed my driver's test—it took me only six tries.

_____ 10. My <u>contentment</u> was complete as I nestled under the blanket with a good book and a cup of cocoa.

5 A good way to remember word parts is to pick one word that uses a word part and understand how that word part functions in the word. Then you can apply that meaning to other words that have the same word part. Use the words to help you match the word part to its meaning.

SET ONE

_____ 1. –ten–: intention, contention, extend

_____ 2. –ment: assessment, contentment, resentment

_____ 3. inter–: interactive, international, intervene

_____ 4. –chron–: chronological, chronic, synchronize

_____ 5. –man–, -manu–: manuscript, manually, management

a. action, state of being

b. between, among

c. time

d. hand

e. to stretch

SET TWO

_____ 6. –or, -er: counselor, philosopher, interviewer   f. away from, not

_____ 7. pre-: predict, preview, pretend   g. condition, act of

_____ 8. –dic-, -dict-: predict, dictionary, dictation   h. one who

_____ 9. –tion, -ation: opposition, graduation, congratulations   i. before

_____ 10. dis-: disorganized, discourage, dislike   j. to say, to tell, to use words

6 Use the dictionary to find a word you don't know that uses the word part. Write the meaning of the word part, the word, and the definition. If your dictionary has the etymology (history) of the word, see how the word part relates to the meaning, and write the etymology after the definition.

Word Part	Meaning	Word	Definition and Etymology
EXAMPLE:			
-chron-	time	chronograph	an instrument that graphically records time intervals such as the length of an event. Chrono- (time) + -graph (written)
1. pre-			
2. man-			
3. dis-			

4. *inter-* _____

   _____

   _____

   _____

5. *dict-* _____

   _____

   _____

   _____

5 Collecting

Finding a Treasure

Collectibles Show

Saturday March 7, 2004
Youtsey Hall at the Fairgrounds
9 am – 7 pm

Buy ◆ *Sell* ◆ *Share*   5

Remarkable treasures to be found!

Exhibits will **reflect** all **aspects** of collecting, from ways to display your
items to lectures on how to find those **elusive** pieces.

Impartial appraisers will be on hand to check the **authenticity** of your
purchases or an item from your home in order to have its value **verified**.   10

Meet people with similar interests. Food and drink will be available.

No need to seek elsewhere!
Find vendors selling a variety of items:

exquisite Victorian glass ornaments ◆ rare stamps and coins
one-of-a-kind thimbles ◆ hard-to-find license plates ◆ beautiful dolls   15
cuddly teddy bears ◆ delightful music boxes ◆ unique snow globes
sports **memorabilia** including baseball cards and autographs
and so much more!

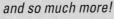

Admission: $10

Contact: (555) 360-1450   20
for information on selling

Make a day of it!

Predicting

Circle the definition that best fits each vocabulary word. If you have difficulty, return to the reading on page 27, and underline any context clues you find. After you've made your predictions, check your answers against the Word List below. Place a checkmark in the boxes next to the words whose definitions you missed. These are the words you'll want to study closely.

NOTE: You may want to cover the Word List below with a piece of paper so you don't accidentally see the definitions as you do the Predicting exercise.

☐ 1. **remarkable** (line 6)
   a. common
   b. great
   c. average

☐ 2. **reflect** (line 7)
   a. to mirror
   b. to throw out
   c. to miss

☐ 3. **aspects** (line 7)
   a. lines
   b. parts
   c. lectures

☐ 4. **elusive** (line 8)
   a. causing to remember
   b. making one sick
   c. tending to avoid

☐ 5. **impartial** (line 9)
   a. fair
   b. mean
   c. crazy

☐ 6. **appraisers** (line 9)
   a. people who hand out food
   b. people who sell coins
   c. people who judge the value of things

☐ 7. **authenticity** (line 9)
   a. the quality of being fake
   b. the quality of being real
   c. the quality of being ill

☐ 8. **verified** (line 10)
   a. confirmed
   b. denied
   c. simplified

☐ 9. **exquisite** (line 14)
   a. quickly done
   b. worn out
   c. beautifully made

☐ 10. **memorabilia** (line 17)
   a. things worth doing
   b. places worth visiting
   c. things worth remembering

Word List

appraiser [ə prāz′ ûr]	*n.*	a person who judges the value or quality of a thing
appraise [ə prāz′]	*v.*	to evaluate; to judge
aspect [as′ pekt′]	*n.*	1. a characteristic to be considered; a part; a phase 2. appearance to the eye or the mind; look 3. a facial expression
authenticity [ô′ then tis′ ə tē]	*n.*	the quality of being genuine or real
elusive [i loo′ siv]	*adj.*	tending to avoid or escape understanding or reach
exquisite [eks′ kwi zit]	*adj.*	1. beautifully made 2. so beautiful as to cause happiness 3. intense

impartial [im par′ shəl]	*adj.*	fair; unprejudiced
memorabilia [mem′ ər ə bil′ ē ə, bil′ yə]	*n.*	things worth remembering
reflect [ri flekt′]	*v.*	1. to mirror 2. to show as a result of what one does 3. to think seriously 4. to bend back from a surface
remarkable [ri mär′ kə bəl]	*adj.*	great; amazing; uncommon; rare
verify [ver′ ə fī′]	*v.*	to prove the truth of; to confirm

Self-Tests

I For Set One match each term with its synonym. For Set Two match each term with its antonym.

SYNONYMS
SET ONE

_____ 1. reflect   a. escape

_____ 2. aspect   b. realness

_____ 3. elusive   c. mirror

_____ 4. authenticity   d. judge

_____ 5. appraise   e. phase

HINT

If you get stuck on one question, go to the next one. When you finish answering the ones that are easy for you, see which questions and words are left. With fewer choices the answers should be easier to find.

ANTONYMS
SET TWO

_____ 6. remarkable   f. prejudiced

_____ 7. memorabilia   g. ugly

_____ 8. impartial   h. common

_____ 9. exquisite   i. forgettable

_____ 10. verify   j. deny

2 Circle the word that best completes each sentence.

1. I wasn't sure about the (aspect, authenticity) of the painting I bought, so I took it to an appraiser who specializes in artwork from the eighteenth century.

2. The Tennessee state quarter I have been looking for has proved to be quite (elusive, impartial).

3. For something printed three hundred years ago, the quality of the book is (impartial, remarkable).

4. I collect (appraisers, memorabilia) related to silent movies.

5. The vase is (elusive, exquisite); the glass sparkles.

6. I tried to be (impartial, remarkable), but deep inside I really wanted my former high school to win the championship.

7. I want to (verify, reflect) your address, so I can send you a postcard.

8. Every (authenticity, aspect) of the play disappointed me, from the acting to the scenery.

9. This past weekend doesn't (reflect, appraise) my usual behavior; I rarely stay out until three in the morning.

10. I am going to (appraise, verify) the condition of my neighbor's VCR. She can't decide whether it is worth fixing or if she should just get a new one.

3 Answer the questions about each example. Use each word once.

1. A diamond ring is valued at four thousand dollars. What is the person who makes this judgment called? _____

2. Karl calls the store to confirm that it is open. What does he want to do? _____

3. A ninety-year-old man runs a marathon. What would most people call his achievement? _____

4. Eric thinks about all his options before he picks between two job openings. What is he taking the time to do? _____

5. A hamster has avoided being caught for two weeks. What has the hamster proven to be? _____

6. Connie buys a vase made by a master Italian glass blower. What word would people likely use to describe the vase? _____

7. Citizens consider Judge Creston to be fair; they say he listens to all the facts before making a decision. What kind of judge would they say he is? _____

8. Kris watched as the famous artist created the painting. What would he be able to assure people of? _____

9. Robert saved his ticket stub and an autographed football from the game. What does he collect? _____

10. The way the hotel looked scared away most tourists: the paint was peeling and several windows were broken. What is keeping people from going to the hotel? _____

Vocabulary List

verify

elusive

remarkable

appraiser

reflect

impartial

exquisite

aspect

memorabilia

authenticity

4 Complete the following story by using the vocabulary words. Use each word once.

Melody and Tom enter the Collectibles Show. Melody is looking for music
(1) _____. She especially wants to find a Beatles lunch box and an Elvis Presley poster. Tom likes to collect items that relate to his interests in art and history. Shortly after they arrive, they split up to cover more of the show.

Tom finds a painting of Lewis and Clark's journey on the Missouri. The colors in the sunset are gorgeous, and the bison are painted with incredible detail. Tom considers the painting (2)_____. The seller says he was told it was painted in the 1800's, but he doesn't know by whom. He doesn't try to persuade Tom; he says he likes to be (3)_____. Tom (4)_____ on the man's statements. He isn't sure whether the painting is old or not, but he chooses to buy it anyway.

Tom then decides he wants to (5)_____ when the painting was done. He gets in line to have an (6)_____ from one of the local art galleries

Vocabulary List

remarkable

verify

elusive

appraiser

authenticity

memorabilia

impartial

aspect

exquisite

reflects

evaluate the painting. The woman tells Tom that the painting is definitely from the 1800's done by a little known but well respected artist. Having the (7)_____ of the painting confirmed makes Tom feel better. He is proud to own a genuine piece of history.

Meanwhile, Melody finds a rare Elvis Presley record at a bargain price. She can't believe her luck; it is a (8)_____ discovery. She quickly buys the record and a slightly torn poster of Elvis in one of his white jumpsuits.

When Melody and Tom meet at the end of the day, she can tell by his (9)_____ that he has found a treasure. Melody is also happy although the Beatles lunch box proved to be (10)_____.

Interactive Exercise

Answer the following questions in the spaces provided.

1. What are two items one would likely get appraised?

   _____   _____

2. What is something you would like to own that you think is exquisite?

   _____

3. What kind of memorabilia do you collect or would you like to collect?

   _____

4. What is it hard for you to be impartial about? _____

5. What item in your bedroom reflects your interests or hobbies? _____

6. How would you verify the authenticity of a friend's statement that he has a collection of over one thousand books?

   _____

7. What aspect of collecting appeals to you or do you think might appeal to you?

   _____

8. What is something that you have found to be remarkable? _____

9. What is something that has been elusive in your life? _____

The Slide Show

"As you all know traveling is my favorite hobby. I am so glad you've come to see the slides from my most recent trip. I was going to show them in **chronological** order, but I decided time order wasn't the best way. I traveled back and forth to several islands in Hawaii, so I am going to show one island at a time. This first slide is in Oahu. The people are so **congenial**. You can see my necklace made of flowers, which is called a "lei" in Hawaii, that I was given upon arrival. I love to explore the **cultural** aspects of the places I visit." 5

10

"Here I am **immersed** in Hawaiian traditions as I try the hula. I feel it is **vital** to understand people's traditions. Most people appreciate my **unbridled** enthusiasm, though there are times I need someone to **intercede** when I get too excited." 15

"In this picture I am climbing a tree to get a coconut. The man who owned the tree didn't understand my desire to practice ancient food gathering techniques. It is **inevitable** that I run into some kind of problem when I travel and that is why I always try to **retain** my sense of humor." 20

25

"That is also why it is essential that I have such a **compatible** travel companion as May. We get along so well. Here she is sipping a drink on the beach after calming the man who owned the tree." 30

Predicting

Circle the definition that best fits each vocabulary word. If you have difficulty, return to the reading on page 32, and underline any context clues you find. After you've made your predictions, check your answers against the Word List below. Place a checkmark in the boxes next to the words whose definitions you missed. These are the words you'll want to study closely.

Note: You may want to cover the Word List below with a piece of paper so you don't accidentally see the definitions as you do the Predicting exercise.

❑ 1. **chronological** (line 3)
   a. order of importance
   b. time order
   c. spatial order

❑ 2. **congenial** (line 7)
   a. friendly
   b. mean
   c. lazy

❑ 3. **cultural** (line 10)
   a. relating to moving
   b. relating to death
   c. relating to the ways of life of a group

❑ 4. **immersed** (line 11)
   a. danced
   b. surrounded
   c. ignored

❑ 5. **vital** (line 13)
   a. important
   b. silly
   c. hungry

❑ 6. **unbridled** (line 14)
   a. trapped
   b. cautious
   c. free

❑ 7. **intercede** (line 16)
   a. to request something for another person
   b. to avoid people
   c. to speak when others are talking

❑ 8. **inevitable** (line 22)
   a. incapable of listening
   b. able to avoid
   c. incapable of being prevented

❑ 9. **retain** (line 25)
   a. to give away
   b. to keep
   c. to teach

❑ 10. **compatible** (line 27)
   a. capable of being in an agreeable situation
   b. unable to get along with anyone
   c. unsure of how to act with strangers

Word List

chronological [kron′ ə lo′ ji kəl]	*adj.* arranged in order of time; sequential	**immerse** [i mûrs′]	*v.* to surround; to absorb
compatible [kəm pat′ ə bəl]	*adj.* 1. capable of being in an agreeable situation with others 2. capable of efficient operation with other elements	**inevitable** [in ev′ ə tə bəl]	*adj.* incapable of being prevented; unavoidable; certain
		intercede [in′ tər sēd′]	*v.* to request something for someone else
congenial [kən jēn′ yəl]	*adj.* friendly; pleasant; agreeable	**retain** [rē tān′]	*v.* to keep; to remember
cultural [kul′ chər əl]	*adj.* 1. relating to the different ways of life of a group of people 2. relating to intellectual and artistic activities	**unbridled** [un brīd′ dəld]	*adj.* free; unrestricted
		vital [vī′ təl]	*adj.* important; essential

Self-Tests

1 For Set One and Set Two below, finish the analogies. See the Analogies Appendix on page 143 for instructions and practice.

SET ONE

1. doubt : believe :: _____
2. feelings : unbridled :: _____
3. congenial : pleasant :: _____
4. an explorer : compass :: _____
5. controlling : boss :: _____

a. a writer : chronological
b. compatible : companion
c. laughter : contagious
d. inevitable : avoidable
e. hard : difficult

SET TWO

6. immerse : plunge :: _____
7. laugh : joke :: _____
8. ballet : cultural :: _____
9. study : retain :: _____
10. dark : light :: _____

f. soccer : sport
g. sleep : rested
h. unimportant : vital
i. escort : accompany
j. intercede : argument

2 The following are comments overheard on trips around the world. Finish each sentence using the vocabulary words below. Use each word once.

1. "We are so _____; it's great that we both love to sleep in late."

2. "Let me _____; I speak Italian. Can you direct them to the Washington Monument?"

3. "I have made a _____ list of my plans for tomorrow: first I will go to the Louvre, followed by lunch at a café, and finally a dinner cruise on the Seine."

4. "It was _____ that we would have at least one argument on a six-week trip together."

5. "I chose to stay with a family because I wanted to _____ myself in the Spanish language while in Mexico."

6. "Our hostess is so _____. She said we should help ourselves to anything we wanted to eat in her kitchen."

7. "I was able to _____ a dozen words of Swedish even after traveling through four other countries."

8. "It is _____ that everyone stays with the tour group; it is easy to get lost in the Imperial Palace."

9. "The _____ festival is being held to celebrate food, dance, and costumes from many countries."

10. "Come on, everyone; get up. My excitement is _____. It's almost six, and we have so much to see and do!"

Vocabulary List

congenial

immerse

unbridled

retain

compatible

cultural

vital

intercede

inevitable

chronological

3 Match each vocabulary word to its definition.

_____ 1. cultural   a. essential

_____ 2. intercede   b. to surround

_____ 3. chronological   c. agreeable with others

_____ 4. inevitable   d. unrestricted

_____ 5. vital   e. to request for another

_____ 6. compatible   f. friendly

_____ 7. immerse   g. to keep

_____ 8. unbridled   h. sequential

_____ 9. congenial   i. unavoidable

_____ 10. retain   j. artistic activities

4 Finish these headlines from the travel section. Use each word once.

Vocabulary List

intercede	inevitable	compatible	unbridled	retain
cultural	vital	immerse	congenial	chronological

1. **Are You and Your Loved Ones _____ Travel Partners?**

2. **Be Prepared: The _____ Long Lines Loom at Amusement Parks this Summer**

3. **_____ Information on How to Protect Your Health Abroad**

4. **Tourists Return from Australia with _____ Enthusiasm for Beauty of the Country**

5. **_____ Your Sanity—Spend a Week on a Greek Island**

6. *Three-Week _____ Tour of China's Museums and Historic Sites*

7. _____ Yourself in the Jungle For Five Days—African Safaris Offer Great Experiences

8. Officials _____ on Behalf of Tour Group Stuck in Border Dispute

9. *Unique _____ Tour of Egypt Takes the Traveler from Ancient to Modern Times*

10. Warm Beaches and _____ People Welcome Travelers to Brazil

Interactive Exercise

LET'S TRAVEL: It's time for a mini-vacation. You have three days and $600 to spend. Decide where you would like to go, and prepare the following items.

1. Select a *compatible* travel companion, and explain why the person will be *congenial* to travel with. _____

2. What is a problem you will *inevitably* run into while planning your trip or while on your trip? Who might be able to *intercede* and help solve the problem? _____
   _____

3. List two areas you have an *unbridled* interest in. How can you *immerse* yourself in one of these interests on your trip? _____ _____
   _____

4. Make a *chronological* list of what you will do each day. List at least two *cultural* activities. Circle the activity you consider *vital* to making your trip a success.

	Day 1	Day 2	Day 3
morning	_____	_____	_____
afternoon	_____	_____	_____
evening	_____	_____	_____

5. What memories do you think you will *retain* from this trip? _____
   _____

7 Computers

A New World

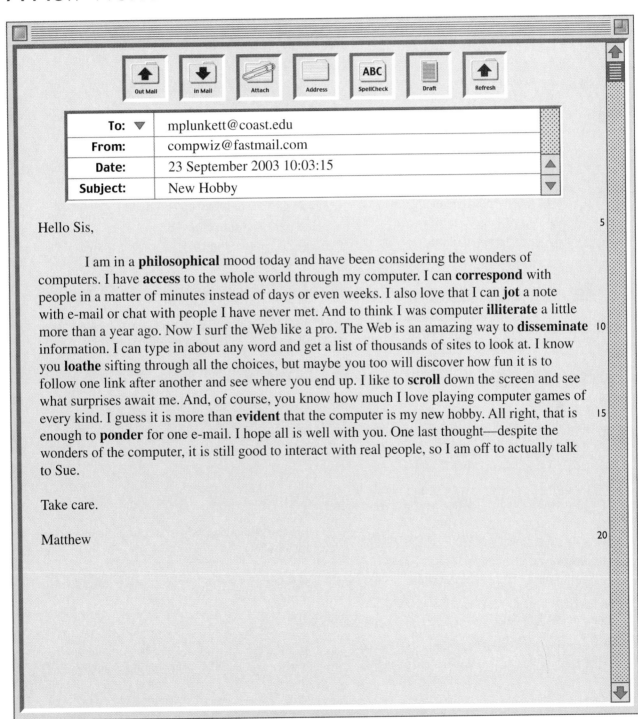

To: ▼	mplunkett@coast.edu
From:	compwiz@fastmail.com
Date:	23 September 2003 10:03:15
Subject:	New Hobby

Hello Sis,   5

    I am in a **philosophical** mood today and have been considering the wonders of
computers. I have **access** to the whole world through my computer. I can **correspond** with
people in a matter of minutes instead of days or even weeks. I also love that I can **jot** a note
with e-mail or chat with people I have never met. And to think I was computer **illiterate** a little
more than a year ago. Now I surf the Web like a pro. The Web is an amazing way to **disseminate** 10
information. I can type in about any word and get a list of thousands of sites to look at. I know
you **loathe** sifting through all the choices, but maybe you too will discover how fun it is to
follow one link after another and see where you end up. I like to **scroll** down the screen and see
what surprises await me. And, of course, you know how much I love playing computer games of
every kind. I guess it is more than **evident** that the computer is my new hobby. All right, that is 15
enough to **ponder** for one e-mail. I hope all is well with you. One last thought—despite the
wonders of the computer, it is still good to interact with real people, so I am off to actually talk
to Sue.

Take care.

Matthew   20

Predicting

Circle the definition that best fits each vocabulary word. If you have difficulty, return to the reading on page 37, and underline any context clues you find. After you've made your predictions, check your answers against the Word List below. Place a checkmark in the boxes next to the words whose definitions you missed. These are the words you'll want to study closely.

NOTE: You may want to cover the Word List below with a piece of paper so you don't accidentally see the definitions as you do the Predicting exercise.

❑ 1. **philosophical** (line 6)
  a. thoughtful
  b. wild
  c. disgusting

❑ 2. **access** (line 7)
  a. the ability to enter
  b. well done
  c. too much

❑ 3. **correspond** (line 7)
  a. to take a walk
  b. to drink
  c. to write someone

❑ 4. **jot** (line 8)
  a. to travel widely
  b. to write quickly
  c. to sleep late

❑ 5. **illiterate** (line 9)
  a. ignorant of the basics
  b. sure of everything
  c. curious

❑ 6. **disseminate** (line 10)
  a. to conceal
  b. to cancel
  c. to spread

❑ 7. **loathe** (line 12)
  a. to hate
  b. to love
  c. to want

❑ 8. **scroll** (line 13)
  a. to stay in one place
  b. to hurry
  c. to move up and down

❑ 9. **evident** (line 15)
  a. confused
  b. clear
  c. busy

❑ 10. **ponder** (line 16)
  a. to swim
  b. to fly
  c. to consider

Word List

access [ak′ ses]	*n.* state of being able to approach or enter *v.* to get	**jot** [jot]	*v.* to write briefly and quickly
correspond [kôr′ ə spond′]	*v.* 1. to communicate by letter, usually over a period of time 2. to be in agreement	**loathe** [lōTH]	*v.* to detest; to hate
disseminate [di sem′ ə nāt′]	*v.* to spread widely; to distribute	**philosophical** [fil′ ə sof′ i kəl]	*adj.* thoughtful; serene; wise
evident [ev′ ə dənt]	*adj.* easily seen; clear	**ponder** [pon′ dər]	*v.* to consider carefully; to reflect
illiterate [i lit′ ər it]	*adj.* 1. ignorant of the basics in an area or subject 2. unable to read and write	**scroll** [skrōl]	*v.* to move up and down on a computer screen *n.* a roll of paper with writing on it

Self-Tests

Complete the sentences below using the vocabulary words. Use each word once.

1. I was _____ about not winning the debate.

2. It's 7:20, and my appointment is at 7:30 twenty miles away. It is _____ that I will not make it there on time.

3. I will take some time to _____ whether to change jobs before I make a decision.

4. The knight delivered the _____ to the king.

5. I _____ with my pen pal twice a month.

6. The woman discovered her date was _____ when she saw that he was unable to read a menu.

7. I _____ down my grocery list just before I go to the store.

8. I _____ getting junk mail.

9. I have easy _____ to my client files on the computer.

10. We need to _____ these fliers all over town before the election.

Vocabulary List

ponder

correspond

illiterate

loathe

philosophical

jot

access

disseminate

evident

scroll

In each group, circle the word that does not have a connection to the other three words.

EXAMPLE: write   (ignore)   reply   correspond

When you correspond, you reply or write to a person. *Ignore* is not related to the other words.

1. reflect	ponder	think	do
2. clear	evident	plain	hidden
3. distribute	keep	spread	disseminate
4. jot	list	essay	note
5. detest	love	loathe	hate
6. scroll	message	move	yell
7. illiterate	ignorant	knowledgeable	unable
8. entry	access	blocked	approachable
9. depressed	calm	quiet	philosophical
10. same	correspond	different	agreement

3 Put a T for true or F for false next to each statement.

_____ 1. It only takes a few minutes to jot a novel.

_____ 2. Most people loathe bubble baths after a hard day at work.

_____ 3. People have access to newspapers and libraries on the Web.

_____ 4. Carrier pigeon is an easy way to disseminate information.

_____ 5. It is a good idea to ponder major purchases.

_____ 6. People today often get scrolls in the mail.

_____ 7. E-mail can be a fast way to correspond with friends.

_____ 8. It is evident that technology is important to the entertainment business.

_____ 9. Being illiterate makes it easy to get through college.

_____ 10. It can be relaxing to consider a philosophical quotation before going to bed.

4 Complete the e-mails below by using the vocabulary words. Use each word once. Create the names and information to complete the "To", "From", "Date", and "Subject" lines.

MESSAGE ONE

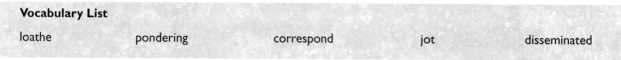

Vocabulary List

loathe   pondering   correspond   jot   disseminated

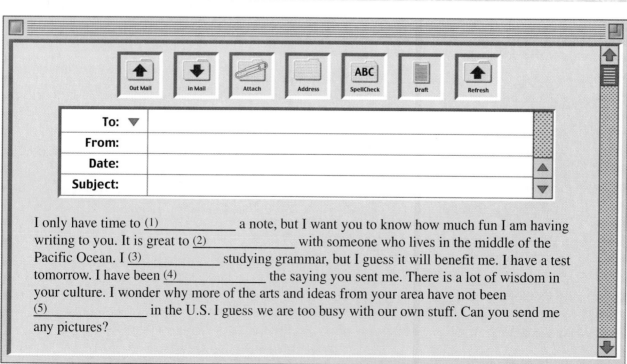

To: ▼

From:

Date:

Subject:

I only have time to (1) _____ a note, but I want you to know how much fun I am having writing to you. It is great to (2) _____ with someone who lives in the middle of the Pacific Ocean. I (3) _____ studying grammar, but I guess it will benefit me. I have a test tomorrow. I have been (4) _____ the saying you sent me. There is a lot of wisdom in your culture. I wonder why more of the arts and ideas from your area have not been (5) _____ in the U.S. I guess we are too busy with our own stuff. Can you send me any pictures?

Vocabulary List

access   illiterate   philosophical   scroll   evident

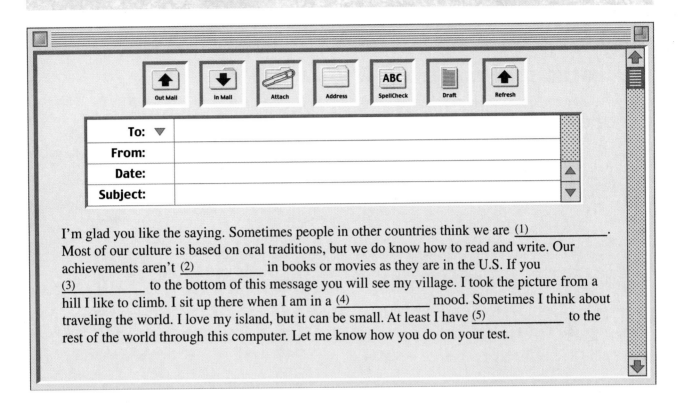

I'm glad you like the saying. Sometimes people in other countries think we are <u>(1)</u>_____.
Most of our culture is based on oral traditions, but we do know how to read and write. Our
achievements aren't <u>(2)</u>_____ in books or movies as they are in the U.S. If you
<u>(3)</u>_____ to the bottom of this message you will see my village. I took the picture from a
hill I like to climb. I sit up there when I am in a <u>(4)</u>_____ mood. Sometimes I think about
traveling the world. I love my island, but it can be small. At least I have <u>(5)</u>_____ to the
rest of the world through this computer. Let me know how you do on your test.

Interactive Exercise

Answer the following questions:

1. What is something you loathe? Why? _____

2. What are three occasions when you might jot something down?

   _____   _____   _____

3. What do you think is the best way to disseminate information? _____

4. What should all people have access to? _____

5. If you could correspond with one famous person, who would it be? _____

6. What was the last decision you had to ponder? _____

7. What area are you illiterate in? _____

8. Where might you find a scroll? _____

9. What are you philosophical about? _____

10. Name one evident way computers have changed the world. _____

8 Review

Focus on Chapters 1–7

1. _____

2. _____

3. _____

4. _____

5. _____

6. _____

7. _____

8. _____

9. _____

10. _____

11. _____

12. _____

The following activities give you a chance to interact some more with the vocabulary words you've been learning. By looking at art, acting, writing, taking tests, and doing a crossword puzzle, you will see which words you know well and which you still need to work with.

Art

Match each picture on page 42 to one of the following vocabulary words. Use each word once.

Vocabulary List

scroll	faculty	exquisite	memorabilia
frazzled	immerse	loathe	collaborative
disorganized	correspond	congenial	orientation

Collaborative Activity: Drama

Charades: You will be given one of the following words to act out in class. Think about how this word could be demonstrated without speaking. The other people in class will try to guess what word you are showing.

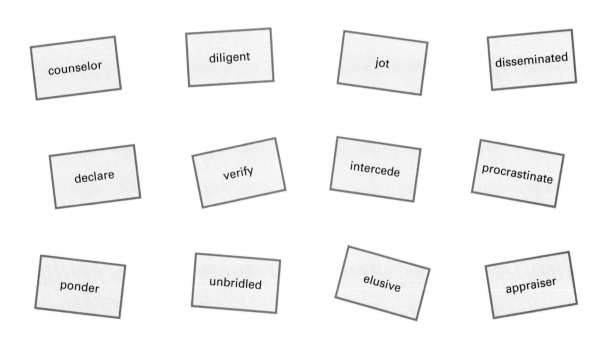

counselor diligent jot disseminated

declare verify intercede procrastinate

ponder unbridled elusive appraiser

Writing

Answer the following questions to further test your understanding of the vocabulary words.

1. Who might need help with phonics? _____

2. What is something you need to take the initiative in? _____
   _____

3. What would you want to check the authenticity of before buying? _____
   _____

4. What is something that uses chronological order? _____
   _____

5. What can you do to overcome being illiterate in something? _____
   _____

6. What is a benefit of being impartial about things? _____
   _____

7. Where would be a good place to sit and be philosophical? Why? _____
   _____

8. What do you have an aptitude for? _____
   _____

9. What things in your life should you take a yearly assessment of? _____
   _____

10. Where might you expect an orientation? _____
   _____

HINT

Learn From Your Mistakes

You will be taking quizzes and tests throughout this course, as well as in other classes. Remember that taking a test is simply another way to learn. You learn what you know and what you don't know. When you get a test back, you should always look at your errors, especially if you receive a low grade. It is normal to feel disappointed, but ask yourself first if you really spent enough time with the words before you took the test. If you didn't, then you know what you need to do next time. Then, *look at every error.* If you don't understand why something is wrong, ask the instructor. Go back to the chapter and study all of the exercises where the word was used.

If you follow these procedures, you will learn from the error and will probably not make the same mistake again. Keep in mind that *the grade is always less important than what you learn.* If you really learn how to use the words, you'll get good grades.

Self-Tests

Finish the story using the vocabulary words below. Use each word once.

Vocabulary List

access	allot	antonyms	context clues	cope
interactive	pondered	procrastinated	remarkable	task

LEARNING WORDS

Matt was afraid to go to college because he did not have a very big vocabulary. His friend Dan, however, told him not to be scared because he could take a class to build his vocabulary skills. Matt (1)_____ what his friend said, and after thinking about it overnight, he decided he would sign up for the class.

On the first day the instructor told the class that the semester would not be difficult if they were willing to study. Matt didn't want to make things hard, so he was ready to (2)_____ several hours a week to doing his assignments. Matt got the book for the class and saw that it was going to be fun to use because it had several (3)_____ exercises. It was great to do activities like art and drama to learn new words. He was going to have to work hard, but he would also enjoy it.

One of the techniques Matt learned first was to look for (4)_____. Those were words around a word that could give him an idea of what the word meant. Matt became an expert at finding these clues. He knew they could come in different forms such as examples, synonyms, or (5)_____. Looking for words that meant the opposite of the word he didn't know was something he had never thought of doing.

On the first quiz Matt got a C. He knew he could have done better if he hadn't (6)_____ and studied only the night before. Matt decided that to (7)_____ with the work he would begin to study his words every day. He now gave at least seven hours a week to the class. On the next test and all the rest, Matt got an A.

At the end of the class, Matt had (8)_____ to a lot of new words. He saw his friend Dan one day, who asked how Matt liked the vocabulary class. Matt told him, "I am no longer frazzled by the (9)_____ of reading college-level books. My vocabulary is now (10)_____, and I can read with confidence." Dan smiled at his friend and nodded in agreement.

2 Pick the word that best completes each sentence.

1. It can be hard for me to make a _____ to exercising, but I do need to make it part of my weekly activities.

   a. task   b. faculty   c. commitment   d. scroll

2. Wendy looked _____ after a car almost ran into her.

   a. frazzled   b. unbridled   c. illiterate   d. impartial

3. The meeting was so _____ no one knew what issue they were voting on.

   a. vital   b. disorganized   c. diligent   d. congenial

4. I want to find a _____ that can lead to a career overseas.

   a. task   b. management   c. major   d. synonym

5. I took the time to _____ on how much I was studying and decided that I need to put more time into my school work if I want to learn anything.

   a. reflect   b. immerse   c. loathe   d. declare

6. It was _____ that my nephew was visiting; I saw a pile of toys as soon as I opened the door.

   a. interactive   b. compatible   c. diligent   d. evident

7. Mary was so _____ at doing her homework that she could relax on the weekends.

   a. exquisite   b. efficient   c. frazzled   d. cultural

8. I didn't think the _____ was doing a good job of training the staff; all of the servers were rude and slow.

   a. counselor   b. appraiser   c. antonym   d. management

9. David had _____ to lots of information after he learned to use the Internet.

   a. access   b. aptitude   c. orientation   d. aspect

10. I want to _____ membership in my gym, so I will continue to pay the dues although I will be gone for over six months.

    a. empower   b. prioritize   c. retain   d. verify

Crossword Puzzle

Use the following words to complete the crossword puzzle. Use each word once.

Vocabulary List

accomplishment

analogy

aspect

collaborative

compatible

cultural

diligent

empower

inevitable

loathe

predict

prioritize

synonyms

theme

vital

Across

3. We will get it done if we work together.
8. When I finish my homework, I feel like I have done this.
11. to enable
12. to study for a test, to eat right, to get plenty of sleep
13. a topic
14. up : down :: slow : fast

Down

1. the ballet, the opera, the symphony
2. what to do first
3. they both enjoy movies, dinners out, and long walks
4. happy, glad, and cheerful
5. to tell before it happens
6. a part or a facial expression
7. People often feel this way about lima beans and liver
9. certain
10. steady and energetic

CHAPTER

9 Art

A Day at the Modern Art Museum

Predicting

Circle the definition that best fits each vocabulary word. If you have difficulty, return to the reading on page 48, and underline any context clues you find. After you've made your predictions, check your answers against the Word List below. Place a checkmark in the boxes next to the words whose definitions you missed. These are the words you'll want to study closely.

NOTE: You may want to cover the Word List below with a piece of paper so you don't accidentally see the definitions as you do the Predicting exercise.

❑ 1. **relevance** (panel 1)
    a. unimportance
    b. importance
    c. a curtain

❑ 2. **alienation** (panel 1)
    a. isolation
    b. togetherness
    c. a big party

❑ 3. **symbolize** (panel 2)
    a. to bang
    b. to remember
    c. to represent

❑ 4. **absurdity** (panel 2)
    a. seriousness
    b. a hard stomach
    c. foolishness

❑ 5. **abstract** (panel 3)
    a. blocked
    b. complex
    c. slim

❑ 6. **desperation** (panel 3)
    a. hopelessness
    b. sweat
    c. happiness

❑ 7. **obviously** (panel 4)
    a. clearly
    b. madly
    c. softly

❑ 8. **futility** (panel 4)
    a. importance
    b. meaninglessness
    c. caution

❑ 9. **gallery** (panel 5)
    a. a greenhouse
    b. a kitchen
    c. an exhibition room

❑ 10. **revelation** (panel 6)
    a. a high place
    b. discovery
    c. something confusing

Word List

abstract
[ab strakt′]
  adj. 1. not easily understood; complex
  2. not practical; an idea not related to a specific example

absurdity
[ab sûr′ di tē]
  n. nonsense; foolishness

alienation
[ā′ lē ə nā′ shən]
  n. division; isolation; distance

desperation
[des′ pə rā′ shən]
  n. hopelessness; sorrow

futility
[fyo͞o til′ ə tē]
  n. emptiness; meaninglessness

gallery
[gal′ ə rē]
  n. exhibition room; hall

obviously
[ob′ vē əs lē]
  adv. clearly; plainly

relevance
[rel′ ə vəns]
  n. significance; importance

revelation
[rev′ ə lā′ shən]
  n. announcement; discovery

symbolize
[sim′ bə līz′]
  v. to represent; to mean

Self-Tests

1 Match the situation to the word it best fits.

SET ONE

—— 1. continuously pushing a rock up a hill and having it roll back

—— 2. not being friends with anyone

—— 3. making a connection between a reading in history and a short story in English

—— 4. considering the possibility of time travel

—— 5. finally understanding how to figure out what X is in an equation

a. alienation

b. revelation

c. futility

d. relevance

e. abstract

SET TWO

—— 6. a student buying a term paper to pass a class

—— 7. walking around a place filled with paintings

—— 8. winking at someone to show you like the person

—— 9. a college scheduling all classes from midnight to five A.M.

—— 10. exchanging rings at a wedding to represent a couple's commitment to each other

f. obvious

g. gallery

h. desperation

i. symbolize

j. absurdity

2 You are lost in the art museum, and you ask several people for directions to the gift shop. Put the correct vocabulary words in the spaces below to help you make sense of their answers. Choose from these words: futile, absurd, alienation, abstract, revelation, relevance, desperate, gallery, obviously, symbolize.

"Walk down this _____ to the painting of the woman with three eyes. This complex picture is at the entrance to the _____ collection. Now turn left. Go past two more paintings, and on your right will be a sculpture of a man with his back to you. He is all alone and shows man's _____ in the modern world. As soon as you go by him, turn right, and go downstairs, and you are there."

"You shouldn't have come down these stairs. What kind of _____ instructions did you get? Oh well, don't look so _____; it isn't really that far now. Go back upstairs and turn right. After you pass the big black painting with the blue circle in the middle, which is supposed to _____ the beginning of life (at least that's what the artist told me), you want to turn left and go down those stairs."

"_____, you have been talking to the wrong people, but don't worry. Your search is not _____. Go down this hall and turn left at the picture of the waterfall; you'll understand the _____ of where this painting is placed when you hear the fountain nearby. It's a great effect to put them near each other. Go past the fountain, turn right, and there will be the wonderful _____: the gift shop."

3 For Set One match each term with its synonym. For Set Two match each term with its antonym.

SYNONYMS
SET ONE

_____ 1. symbolize   a. complex

_____ 2. abstract   b. emptiness

_____ 3. gallery   c. represent

_____ 4. futility   d. discovery

_____ 5. revelation   e. hall

ANTONYMS
SET TWO

_____ 6. alienation   f. hope

_____ 7. obviously   g. insignificance

_____ 8. absurdity   h. hidden

_____ 9. desperation   i. belonging

_____ 10. relevance   j. seriousness

4 Fill in the blanks with the appropriate vocabulary word. Use each word once.

1. I, _____, need some tutoring in math. I got another "D" on a quiz.

2. As I opened the front door, I saw the _____ of trying to keep my yard free of leaves; the wind had blown another bunch down overnight.

3. The _____ of trying to plan a big wedding in a month became more obvious as the day got closer and there were still lots of plans to make.

4. The number of candles on a birthday cake _____ the person's age.

5. Unfortunately, the reception was held in the smallest _____ of the art museum, and we were way too crowded.

6. I didn't understand the _____ of my English professor's lecture on World War II until I started reading the novel for the class and discovered it took place during the war.

7. Clyde's _____ kept him from enjoying the first year of college, but he joined some clubs his second year and felt better.

8. Annette's ideas are often so _____ that I don't understand what she is talking about.

9. My sister's _____ that she was pregnant surprised all of us.

10. Out of _____ Tom stayed up all night studying before the final. He hadn't studied all semester, and now he wasn't sure he would pass.

Vocabulary List

symbolize

revelation

gallery

obviously

absurdity

desperation

futility

relevance

abstract

alienation

Interactive Exercise

In the spaces provided, draw pictures that represent at least three of the vocabulary words.

Word(s): _____

Word(s): _____

Word(s): _____

10 Music

The Interview

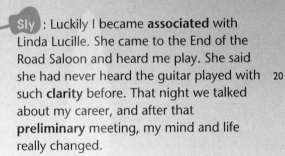

Music Magazine was lucky to get a rare interview with **Sly Wilson** last month before his concert in
5 Nashville.

MM: *There hasn't always been an* ***appreciation*** *of your music, Sly. What do you think has brought people around to your blend of blue grass and jazz?*

10 **Sly** : For a long time I was a **novice** at just getting noticed. I really **jeopardized** my own career by playing in my local bar for years. I never hit the road or tried to record anything.

15 **MM:** *So what brought about your* ***awareness*** *that you needed to change tactics?*

Sly : Luckily I became **associated** with Linda Lucille. She came to the End of the Road Saloon and heard me play. She said she had never heard the guitar played with 20 such **clarity** before. That night we talked about my career, and after that **preliminary** meeting, my mind and life really changed.

MM: *Can you* ***elaborate*** *on how?* 25

Sly : Well, I was always a bit **maladjusted**, so to speak. I never fit in with the rest of my classmates. I just thought it was me. Then Linda took me to Nashville and New Orleans, and I found people who shared 30 my love of music.

MM: *You have been called a* ***visionary***. *Do you think the title fits?*

Sly : I do see music differently from a lot of people, so I guess it does. I think now 35 people are coming around and beginning to share my views of how different sounds can be combined.

Predicting

Circle the definition that best fits each vocabulary word. If you have difficulty, return to the reading on page 53, and underline any context clues you find. After you've made your predictions, check your answers against the Word List below. Place a checkmark in the boxes next to the words whose definitions you missed. These are the words you'll want to study closely.

Note: You may want to cover the Word List below with a piece of paper so you don't accidentally see the definitions as you do the Predicting exercise.

☐ 1. **appreciation** (line 7)
    a. a type of storm
    b. a favorable opinion
    c. a group of people singing

☐ 2. **novice** (line 10)
    a. a beginner
    b. an expert
    c. a painful experience

☐ 3. **jeopardized** (line 11)
    a. helped
    b. risked
    c. eased

☐ 4. **awareness** (line 15)
    a. fear
    b. knowledge
    c. state of exhaustion

☐ 5. **associated** (line 17)
    a. connected with
    b. helping with
    c. staying away from

☐ 6. **clarity** (line 21)
    a. clearness
    b. confusion
    c. darkness

☐ 7. **preliminary** (line 23)
    a. quick
    b. beginning
    c. ending

☐ 8. **elaborate** (line 25)
    a. turn away
    b. stop talking
    c. provide more information

☐ 9. **maladjusted** (line 26)
    a. unable to go
    b. able to sing
    c. unable to conform

☐ 10. **visionary** (line 32)
    a. a person who likes music
    b. a person without ideas
    c. a person who can look ahead

Word List

appreciation
[ə prē′ shē a′ shən]
n. 1. a favorable opinion
2. feeling of thanks
3. recognition of quality
4. an increase in value

associated
[ə so′ shē ā təd, -sē ā təd]
adj. connected; joined in some type of relationship

associate
v. [e so′ shē āt′, -sē āt]
v. to join; to combine
n. [e sō′ shē′ it, -sē it]
n. a partner; a companion

awareness
[ə wâr′ nes]
n. consciousness; knowledge

clarity
[klar′ ə tē]
n. clearness; brightness; easy to understand

elaborate
v. [i lab′ ə rāt′]
adj. [i lab′ ər it]
v. 1. provide more information
2. to work out thoroughly
adj. planned with attention to details; complicated

jeopardize
[jep′ ûr dīz′]
v. to risk; to threaten

maladjusted
[mal′ ə jus′ tid]
adj. 1. unable to conform
2. emotionally unstable
3. not well fitted

novice
[nov′ əs]
n. a beginner

preliminary
[pre lim′ ə nâr′ ē]
adj. beginning; introductory

visionary
[vizh′ ən er′ ē]
n. 1. one with an unusual ability to look ahead; a prophet
2. one given to impractical ideas; a dreamer
adj. not currently possible

Self-Tests

1 For each set, match the quotation to the word it best fits. Context clues are underlined to help you make the connections. Use each word once.

SET ONE

1. "At my <u>introductory</u> meeting with the voice instructor, he said I showed <u>great promise</u>." _____

2. "I don't want <u>to risk</u> hurting my fingers before the big piano recital, so I'll skip the football game." _____

3. "I am a <u>beginner</u> at playing the tuba, so I'm not very good yet."
   _____

4. "Her voice is so <u>clear</u>; I can understand every word of her songs."
   _____

5. "I don't think Mike saw us waving at him. He is probably thinking about some impossible invention he wants to make; he is such a <u>dreamer</u>." _____

Vocabulary List

clarity

novice

visionary

jeopardize

preliminary

SET TWO

6. "I brought you cookies as a <u>sign of thanks</u> for letting me borrow your notes when I was sick." _____

7. "This party is going to be great. I have <u>every detail thoroughly worked out</u>, from the color of the napkins to the games we will play."
   _____

8. "I <u>don't fit in</u> my humanities class. Everyone loves to read dead Romans and debate them, and I can't get excited about them at all."
   _____

9. "I want <u>to join</u> the garden club so I can meet other people who love plants." _____

10. "I <u>know what is going on</u>, but I don't know how to stop the problem."
    _____

Vocabulary List

elaborate

awareness

appreciation

maladjusted

associate

2 Match the vocabulary word to its definition.

_____ 1. awareness	a. to risk
_____ 2. preliminary	b. clearness
_____ 3. appreciation	c. introductory
_____ 4. visionary	d. beginner
_____ 5. clarity	e. feelings of thanks
_____ 6. maladjusted	f. connected
_____ 7. associated	g. a dreamer
_____ 8. jeopardize	h. knowledge
_____ 9. novice	i. complicated
_____ 10. elaborate	j. emotionally unstable

3 Circle the word that correctly completes each sentence.

1. The (novice, clarity) of her writing made it easy to understand her argument.

2. I like to invite Connie to dinner. She has a real (visionary, appreciation) for good food.

3. He (jeopardized, elaborated) his chances of getting into the college he wanted because he forgot to mail his application on time.

4. I consider Marlene a (clarity, visionary); things always turn out as she predicts.

5. The (preliminary, maladjusted) plans for the house didn't look a thing like the completed project.

6. My professor says I need to (elaborate, jeopardize) on my ideas for my papers to make a strong point.

7. My (awareness, associate) and I will be at a meeting in Chicago next week.

8. People say Sarah is (maladjusted, visionary), but she is just shy. Once you get to know her she is quite nice.

9. Kris is supposedly a (clarity, novice) at tennis, but he serves like a pro.

10. An (appreciation, awareness) of why I was in the hospital slowly came to me as I remembered the skiing accident.

4 Complete the story below by using the vocabulary words. Use each word once.

Vocabulary List				
novice	preliminary	jeopardized	elaborate	visionary
awareness	appreciation	clarity	maladjusted	associated

"I'm so depressed."

"What's wrong Sally?"

"I just got back from the (1)_____ interviews for the school symphony, and I don't think it went well."

"What happened?"

"The conductor is a (2)_____; he sees the future of music. I so want to be (3)_____ with him. I think I (4)_____ my chances by drooling on him."

"You didn't really drool on him, did you?"

"No, but I kept expressing my (5)_____ for letting me try out and someone had to finally tap me on the shoulder to get me to sit down. I am just a (6)_____ at the cello, so I don't know what I expected. I had (7)_____ plans for my future. I was going to travel the world playing in famous symphonies."

"Well, maybe you can see your world with a little more (8)_____ now. You are an excellent cello player, but your ideas are a little (9)_____ for your current abilities."

"My (10)_____ is hard won now that I have made a fool of myself."

Ring! Ring!

"Hello. Yes. Yes. Yes! Thank you, thank you so much! Goodbye. Maggie, I'm in!"

Interactive Exercise

Pretend you went to the Sly Wilson concert in Nashville and write a review of it. Use at least seven of the vocabulary words in your review.

_____

_____

_____

_____

_____

_____

_____

_____

_____

_____

_____

_____

_____

_____

_____

_____

_____

_____

_____

_____

HINT

If you feel "writer's block" when doing a writing exercise, try these prewriting techniques:
- Freewriting: Write without stopping for five minutes about your topic. Put down any ideas that come to mind.
- Brainstorming: Write your topic at the top of a piece of paper; then list any words or phrases under it that quickly come to you.
- Clustering: Circle your topic in the middle of a piece of paper. Make lines from it, and fill circles with ideas related to your topic. Again, jot down the ideas.

A Fun Read

The Times

Elaine ON BOOKS

Reviewed by
Elaine Lewis

A *Holiday for Four* is a holiday for reading. If you think reading is a **burden**, this is a book that will make you reconsider your opinion. The writing is witty and the characters are loads of fun. The **predicaments** the characters get into are surprising and the ways they get out of them clever. The book **chronicles** the travels and loves of four twenty-somethings just out of college. There has been a **contention** by some **critics** that the situations are too absurd, but I disagree. There is **sufficient** development of the characters' personalities to believe that they could get themselves into such humorous fixes as getting locked in a castle when they get lost from a tour group. Nothing is **superfluous** in the novel. All the characters and settings are vital to creating this lively tale. If your life is getting **monotonous** take a break and read Adele Oslong's *A Holiday for Four*. It is **fiction** at its best! I can't wait for her next **manuscript** to reach the publisher.

Predicting

Circle the definition that best fits each vocabulary word. If you have difficulty, return to the reading on page 58, and underline any context clues you find. After you've made your predictions, check your answers against the Word List below. Place a checkmark in the boxes next to the words whose definitions you missed. These are the words you'll want to study closely.

NOTE: You may want to cover the Word List below with a piece of paper so you don't accidentally see the definitions as you do the Predicting exercise.

❑ 1. **burden** (line 6)
   a. an easy day
   b. a difficult job
   c. a kind of cheese

❑ 2. **predicaments** (line 11)
   a. carefully worded arguments
   b. difficult or ridiculous situations
   c. long lines

❑ 3. **chronicles** (line 15)
   a. records
   b. jumps
   c. sees

❑ 4. **contention** (line 18)
   a. an agreement
   b. an argument
   c. an invention

❑ 5. **critic** (line 19)
   a. a place in Europe
   b. a person who gives opinions
   c. a person who writes novels

❑ 6. **sufficient** (line 21)
   a. too little
   b. too much
   c. enough

❑ 7. **superfluous** (line 29)
   a. not enough
   b. not the right kind
   c. more than needed

❑ 8. **monotonous** (line 34)
   a. boring
   b. huge
   c. exciting

❑ 9. **fiction** (line 36)
   a. an invented story
   b. a real event
   c. a small part

❑ 10. **manuscript** (line 37)
   a. a fake letter
   b. a check
   c. a document

Word List

burden [bûr′ dən]	*n.* a difficult job, task, or load to carry *v.* to load or overload; to keep down		**fiction** [fik′ shən]	*n.* an invented story; not factual or true
chronicle [kron′ i kəl]	*v.* to record *n.* a chronological record of historical events		**manuscript** [man′ yoo skript]	*n.* a document, generally handwritten
			monotonous [mə not′ ən əs]	*adj.* having no variety; boring
contention [kən ten′ shən]	*n.* 1. an argument 2. a striving to win in competition		**predicament** [pri dik′ ə mənt]	*n.* a difficult, embarrassing, or ridiculous situation
critic [krit′ ik]	*n.* a person who expresses opinions, good or bad, especially about the arts (ex. books, movies, art, music)		**sufficient** [sə fish′ ənt]	*adj.* enough
			superfluous [soo pûr′ floo əs]	*adj.* more than is needed

Self-Tests

1 Complete the sentences using the vocabulary words below. Use each word once.

Vocabulary List				
burdened	critics	monotonous	manuscript	chronicles
contention	fiction	sufficient	predicament	superfluous

1. _____ comment on the sets in a play, as well as the plot and acting.

2. All the sentences are the same pattern, and the writer keeps using the same words over and over. I don't want to read another word of this _____ book.

3. I was in _____ to win the race until I tripped and broke my nose.

4. The author's _____ was turned down two hundred times before it was published.

5. I bought a clock and most of the packaging was _____. It didn't need to be wrapped in five layers.

6. My English professor has _____ me by assigning an entire novel to read and three essays to write in the next two weeks.

7. This book _____ how the Roman Empire fell apart.

8. My _____ is how to get to class now that my car won't start.

9. I have _____ time to write my paper if I start today.

10. I could tell your story about sitting inside all day studying was _____. Hide the sweaty t-shirt and fast-food containers next time to make it believable.

2 Use the vocabulary words to complete these analogies. See the Analogies Appendix on page 143 for instructions and practice.

Vocabulary List				
burden	monotonous	sufficient	contention	predicament
chronicles	critic	manuscript	superfluous	fiction

1. true : false ::

   fact : _____

2. upset : worried ::

   enough : _____

3. song : composer ::

   review : _____

4. sculptor : statue ::

   writer : _____

5. war : peace ::

   harmony : _____

6. slow : fast ::

   lighten : _____

7. zebra : animal ::

one's head stuck in a fence : ＿＿＿＿＿＿＿＿

8. rain : picnic cancelled ::

historical events : ＿＿＿＿＿＿＿＿

9. small : little ::

extra : ＿＿＿＿＿＿＿＿

10. boring : stimulating ::

exciting : ＿＿＿＿＿＿＿＿

3 Match the vocabulary word to its synonym.

＿＿＿＿ 1. contention   a. document

＿＿＿＿ 2. burden   b. difficulty

＿＿＿＿ 3. monotonous   c. unnecessary

＿＿＿＿ 4. sufficient   d. record

＿＿＿＿ 5. fiction   e. reviewer

＿＿＿＿ 6. predicament   f. argument

＿＿＿＿ 7. critic   g. dull

＿＿＿＿ 8. chronicle   h. load

＿＿＿＿ 9. manuscript   i. enough

＿＿＿＿ 10. superfluous   j. untrue

4 Finish the reviews from the backs of fictitious books. Use each word once.

Vocabulary List

monotonous	fiction	chronicles	sufficient	manuscript
burdened	superfluous	contention	critics	predicaments

1. "Rosenquist's first ＿＿＿＿＿＿＿＿ is a gem! This is a writer who will go far."
—*Charleston Sun*

2. "Nothing ＿＿＿＿＿＿＿＿ in a Dickens' novel! Every character–all twenty–are needed to keep this tangled tale going." —*The London Gazette*

3. "A must read! As embarrassing as Penelope's ＿＿＿＿＿＿＿＿ are, she keeps going until she solves the case....She is a detective I want to meet." —*The Village Rag*

4. "There isn't＿＿＿＿＿＿＿＿ room in this column to sing the praises of *The Apartment Next Door*. ...Why did the novel have to end?" —*The Norman Times*

5. "Derby McDermish has lived in the same house for fifty years, he has the same breakfast, lunch and dinner every day, and he owns two pairs of pants–both brown. Only Austen could make such a _____ character funny. ...Cheers for Austen and McDermish!" —*The Newark Star*

6. "Where does fact end and _____ begin in Jackson's novel about the sinking of the Lusitania? Something to ponder. ...worth reading." —*The Yearly News*

7. "Emma Garcia feels _____ with four kids, an unemployed husband, a nosey mother, and a boss who expects perfection. And then she meets a stranger. ...An engrossing look into one woman's personal journey." —*Brownsville Examiner*

8. "*The Invasion* _____ examines attacks and attackers from the Vikings to Vietnam. A must read for any fan of history." —*History Alive*

9. "The _____ agree that Stevenson knows what he's doing. Every novel out does the last! Enjoy!" —*Morro Mirror*

10. "A collection of short stories this good is rare. *The German Immigrant* will certainly be in _____ for some notable awards this year. ...remarkable work..." —*Binghamton Press*

Interactive Exercise

Answer the following questions:

1. Name a burden in your life. _____

2. Name something that has been a point of contention between you and a friend.

   _____

3. What field of art or entertainment would you like to be a critic for? Why? _____

   _____

4. What is one of your favorite works of fiction? _____

5. Name something that you find monotonous. _____

6. Name a predicament you have been involved in. _____

7. What historical event would you like to chronicle? _____

8. What is something one needs sufficient time to do? _____

9. What would you like to write a manuscript about? _____

10. Think of a gathering you have attended. What items were superfluous? _____

   _____

12 Movies

Movie Favorites

Dear Joe,

Did you see they came out with another one of those 100 Greatest Movies Ever list? The magazines give those lists so much **hype** and then they run a TV special about the list. I love movies, but

5 there is too much publicity for these things, especially when the lists have been so lame. I don't want to argue with this latest one too much, but I would never put <u>Rocky</u> on my top 100. Come on. The plot was so **contrived**. I knew he was going to win.

As movie **buffs**, we need to **generate** our own list. We also need

10 some other **categories**. How about the ten most **villainous** characters ever? Definitely on my list is the Wicked Witch of the West in <u>The Wonderful Wizard of Oz</u>. She's so mean! I can already predict who you will have on your list—Darth Vader. If you can pick anything from <u>Star Wars</u>, you will. What about the biggest **blunders** in movie

15 history? Remaking <u>Godzilla</u> certainly **qualifies**. That movie was awful. What is your favorite opening **sequence** for a movie? One of mine is from <u>High Noon</u>. I love watching the horses run and wondering what's going to happen. And, of course, the music is great. What other areas should we include in our **superlative** movie lists?

Write me back soon.

20 Your friend,
Roger

Predicting

Circle the definition that best fits each vocabulary word. If you have difficulty, return to the reading on page 63, and underline any context clues you find. After you've made your predictions, check your answers against the Word List below. Place a checkmark in the boxes next to the words whose definitions you missed. These are the words you'll want to study closely.

NOTE: You may want to cover the Word List below with a piece of paper so you don't accidentally see the definitions as you do the Predicting exercise.

☐ 1. **hype** (line 4)
  a. a walk
  b. excess promotion
  c. something missing

☐ 2. **contrived** (line 8)
  a. real
  b. great
  c. fake

☐ 3. **buff** (line 9)
  a. a song
  b. an admirer
  c. a lazy person

☐ 4. **generate** (line 9)
  a. to start up
  b. to finish
  c. to file

☐ 5. **category** (line 10)
  a. a group
  b. a scary cat
  c. a small room

☐ 6. **villainous** (line 10)
  a. evil
  b. kind
  c. weak

☐ 7. **blunder** (line 14)
  a. a mistake
  b. opposite of lightning
  c. eye covering

☐ 8. **qualify** (line 15)
  a. to be thrown out
  b. to meet the requirements
  c. to run wild

☐ 9. **sequence** (line 16)
  a. without any order
  b. a type of fruit
  c. a logical order

☐ 10. **superlative** (line 19)
  a. a low tone
  b. a hero
  c. an exaggerated expression

Word List

blunder [blun′ dûr]	*n.* a mistake *v.* to make a mistake		**hype** [hīp]	*n.* excess promotion
buff [buf]	*n.* an admirer; a follower		**qualify** [kwäl′ ə fī′]	*v.* to meet the requirements
category [kat′ ə gôr′ ē]	*n.* a class, group, or division		**sequence** [sē′ kwəns]	*n.* arrangement in a logical order
contrived [kən trīvd′]	*adj.* lacking spontaneity; artificial; fake		**superlative** [soo pûr′ lə tiv]	*n.* an exaggerated expression, usually of praise
generate [jen′ ə rāt′]	*v.* to start up; to develop		**villainous** [vil′ ə nəs]	*adv.* evil; very wicked

Self-Tests

© 2004 Pearson Education, Inc.

1 Circle the correct meaning of each word.

1. **hype:**   ignore   go on about

2. **villainous:**   behave badly   do good

3. **blunder:**   perfect   make a mistake

4. **generate:**   create   finish

5. **contrived:**   fake   true

6. **category:**   a logical group   doesn't fit anywhere

7. **qualify:**   has the skill   hasn't a clue

8. **sequence:**   first this, then this   random

9. **buff:**   excited about   couldn't care less

10. **superlative:**   greatest   nice enough

2 Finish the following story using the vocabulary words. Use each word once.

Vocabulary List

villainous	superlatives	category	generate	blunders
buffs	contrived	hype	sequence	qualify

Julie and Diana decide to go to the movies on Saturday night. As they approach the multiplex, finishing their sodas from the James Bond cups they got at the fast food restaurant, they notice another huge billboard for the new Bond movie. They are so tired of the (1)_____ for this film. Julie and Diana won't be seeing the Bond film because they are romance (2)_____. They can't wait to see the picture about a woman who finds love while traveling in South America.

They sit down just in time for the beginning. From a distance the camera shows a boat slowly sailing down the Amazon at sunset. Then the camera comes in closer to show a blond woman in a white evening dress, boa, and a huge jewel-studded necklace walking toward one of the cabins. Finally, she enters the cabin, and the door closes behind her. Julie and Diana are impressed with the opening (3)_____.

A dark-haired woman exits the cabin moments later with an evil look in her eye. She is holding a gun and a large emerald. She quickly puts both of them in a bag. She signals to a small boat close by and disappears in it. Someone yells, "Murder!" It is clear to Julie and Diana that she is a (4)_____ character.

Sandra Bullet, a private detective, rushes out of her cabin. At the same time, two doors down, Antonio Dashing thrusts open his door. Julie whispers to Diana, "These two certainly belong in the good-looking (5)_____."

Sandra and Antonio meet at the murdered woman's door. Antonio stares appreciatively at Sandra, but stops her from entering. "I'm with the Secret Service, and I don't want any (6)_____ made here," he tells her.

Sandra explains, "I'm a detective; I (7)_____ for this job. I'm good–very good—at what I do."

Antonio looks at her and nods, "I'm sure you are. Please join me in solving this case."

Diana whispers to Julie, "This relationship is going to (8)_____ some heat." Julie nods.

As the movie progresses, Sandra and Antonio work together to find the missing emerald of the Incas and end up falling in love. When the movie is over, Julie gushes, "That was the greatest love story I have ever seen. There are so many (9)_____ I could use to describe this film." Diana, on the other hand, declares, "Give me a break! It was easy to tell where they were going to find the jewel, how they were going to get it back, and when they were going to go to bed. It was all so (10)_____."

3 Put a T for true or F for false next to each statement.

_____ 1. Traveling for miles to go to a film festival every weekend would be a sign that one is a movie buff.

_____ 2. Placing a full-page ad in the local paper for a new movie is an example of hype.

_____ 3. People don't need to qualify for the Olympics; anyone can show up and compete.

_____ 4. Getting a perfect score on a test is usually considered a blunder.

_____ 5. It can help to talk to other people to generate ideas about a topic.

_____ 6. "The best issue ever" is a superlative statement.

_____ 7. Baking cookies to share with co-workers would be considered villainous by most people.

_____ 8. Putting a cake in the oven and then pulling it out after ten minutes to add the eggs is the usual baking sequence.

_____ 9. Music stores are rarely organized by categories like jazz, pop, and country.

_____ 10. In movies, when a girl drops her books in front of a boy she likes, the accident is usually contrived.

4 Complete the sentences using the vocabulary words below. Use each word once.

Vocabulary List				
qualify	buff	hype	contrived	generate
categories	sequence	blunder	villainous	superlatives

1. A mascot's job is to _____ excitement in the crowd.

2. "Up, up, down, up, up, down" is an example of a _____.

3. Kidnapping is considered a _____ action.

4. A person usually needs to _____ to be on a swim team.

5. Forgetting to bring one's homework to class would be a _____.

6. Verda is a music _____; she goes to concerts five nights a week.

7. Romance, mystery, and science fiction are examples of _____ one would find in a bookstore.

8. The company really tried to _____ the movie with billboards all over town, constant ads on television, and toys at fast-food chains.

9. Julio raved about my cooking: "Fantastic! Magnificent! The best pasta I have ever had." I appreciated the _____ even if I wasn't sure they were true.

10. Betson called in sick with a sore thumb. Although his excuse sounded _____, his boss told him to take the day off and come in when his thumb felt better.

Interactive Exercise

Generate two responses for each of the following:

Most *Villainous* Characters in a Movie	Most *Contrived* Scenes	Most *Hyped* Movies
1. _____	1. _____	1. _____
2. _____	2. _____	2. _____
Favorite Opening *Sequence* in a Movie	**What *Qualifies* You to Judge Movies**	**Movies in the Action *Category***
1. _____	1. _____	1. _____
2. _____	2. _____	2. _____
Often-Used *Superlatives* About Movies	**Types of Movie *Buff* You Are**	**Biggest Movie *Blunders***
1. _____	1. _____	1. _____
2. _____	2. _____	2. _____

13

Word Parts II

Look for words with these **prefixes**, **roots**, and/or **suffixes** as you work through this book. You may have already seen some of them, and you will see others in later chapters. Learning basic word parts can help you figure out the meanings of unfamiliar words.

prefix: a word part added to the beginning of a word that changes the meaning of the root
root: a word's basic part with its essential meaning
suffix: a word part added to the end of a word; indicates the part of speech

WORD PART	MEANING	EXAMPLES AND DEFINITIONS
Prefixes		
in-, im-, il-, ir-	in, into, on	*intention:* plan to do *impress:* have an impact on
in-, im-, il-, ir-	not	*invincible:* not able to be hurt *immovable:* not able to move; set
mal-	bad, wrong, ill	*malicious:* wanting to do wrong; full of malice *malfunction:* working badly
Roots		
-clar-	clear	*clarify:* to make a point clear *declare:* to state clearly
-gen-	birth, creation	*generate:* to create something *generous:* willing to give or share
-lab-	work	*collaborative:* working together *laboratory:* a workshop for scientific experiments
-scrib-, -script-	write	*manuscript:* a handwritten document *scribble:* to write quickly
Suffixes		
-able, -ible (makes an adjective)	capable of	*remarkable:* capable of being noticed *possible:* capable of being done
-ive (makes an adjective)	performing an action	*interactive:* the action of making connections *decorative:* the action of decorating or looking nice
-ness (makes a noun)	state of being	*awareness:* the state of being aware or knowing *sadness:* the state of being sad or unhappy

Self-Tests

1 Read each definition and choose the appropriate word. Use each word once. The meaning of the word part is underlined to help you make the connection. Refer to the Words Parts list if you need help.

Vocabulary List

productive	manuscript	malnourished	collaborate	courageousness
inspect	illogical	clarify	generate	invincible

1. the <u>action</u> of making something   _____

2. the <u>state of being</u> brave   _____

3. to look <u>into</u> something   _____

4. <u>to</u> create something   _____

5. suffering from <u>bad</u> nutrition   _____

6. <u>not</u> capable of being hurt   _____

7. to make <u>clear</u>   _____

8. <u>not</u> logical   _____

9. <u>work</u> together   _____

10. a <u>written</u> document   _____

2 Finish the sentences with the meaning of each word part. Use each meaning once. The word part is underlined to help you make the connection.

Vocabulary List

clear	workers	creation	write	capable of
bad	not	into	state of being	performing an action

1. <u>Labor</u> Day honors _____.

2. My <u>in</u>tention was to become a lawyer. I wanted to go _____ law to help others.

3. The plan was <u>ir</u>regular because we usually meet at one o'clock and _____ at two.

4. It is <u>im</u>possible for me to attend the meeting at 6 A.M.; I am not _____ getting up that early.

5. When something <u>mal</u>functions, it goes _____.

6. The _____ sad is called sad<u>ness</u>.

Vocabulary List

clear	workers	creation	write	capable of
bad	not	into	state of being	performing an action

7. Her <u>gen</u>erous nature led to the _____ of the fund to help students buy books.

8. He <u>scri</u>bbled the note on the back of an envelope. He would later _____ it on a piece of paper.

9. The candidate de<u>clar</u>ed he was going to run for office; he made his position _____ to everyone.

10. The decor<u>ativ</u>e hanging is _____ of making the room more cheerful.

3 Finish the story using the word parts below. Use each word part once. Your knowledge of word parts, as well as the context clues, will help you create the correct words. If you do not understand the meaning of a word you have made, check the dictionary for the definition or to see whether the word exists.

Word Parts

in	clar	able	ive	mal
lab	gen	scribe	im	ness

THE HAPPY HORROR

I don't know how to de_____ the night I had last night. I awoke when I heard a strange noise. At first I thought it was the wind, but that idea turned out to be _____accurate. It was something more _____evolent or so I thought at first. It was my great-grandfather's ghost. He had been a _____orer; he worked in the fields of our old farm. I had been studying my family's _____eal-ogy, and I had come across a picture of him in a scrapbook. He was a very _____pressive man. He was tall and had an angry face. With much firm_____ I asked him what he wanted with me. He told me he had come back for "a special reason." I asked for some _____ification of that statement. He told me that he found me to be an admir_____ person and that I was the only member of the family he could trust. He said I wouldn't find what I had to do offens_____; he said I would likely enjoy it. After digging in the backyard for an hour, I found the thousand dollars he had hid, and he disappeared when I smiled at him.

4 Pick the best definition for each underlined word using your knowledge of word parts. Circle the word part in each of the underlined words.

a. capable of being true

b. ill smelling

c. a coming in

d. hard to find

e. not capable of being trusted

f. state of having warm feelings

g. a formal statement

h. taking long, hard work

i. the creation of something

j. a message at the end of a letter

_____ 1. My fondness for my aunt goes back to my childhood when she took me to the park to play.

_____ 2. The *Declaration of Independence* clearly stated the views of the American colonies toward England.

_____ 3. The genesis of the idea for Sarah's surprise party came from Sarah herself.

_____ 4. It is probable that I will be late to the meeting because I am coming from across town, and the traffic is bad at noon.

_____ 5. The babysitter's actions were irresponsible—how could she leave a baby alone in a bathtub?

_____ 6. The malodorous air of the basement caused me to step back before entering.

_____ 7. There was an influx of students to the college when the school began to offer more literature courses; students had wanted to read more.

_____ 8. When I tried to find my friend to get the money he owed me, he was very elusive.

_____ 9. It wasn't until the postscript that Karl wrote what time he would arrive.

_____ 10. Making the garage sparkle was a laborious task.

5 A good way to remember word parts is to pick one word that uses a word part and understand how that word part functions in the word. Then you can apply that meaning to other words that have the same word part. Use the words to help you match the word part to its meaning.

SET ONE

_____ 1. –clar-: clarify, clarity, declare

_____ 2. –ive: interactive, supportive, decorative

_____ 3. in-, im-, il-, ir-: invincible, impartial, illiterate

_____ 4. –lab-: collaborative, elaborate, laboratory

_____ 5. mal-: maladjusted, malicious, malfunction

a. work

b. bad, wrong, ill

c. clear

d. not

e. performing an action

SET TWO

_____ 6. –ness: awareness, tenderness, happiness

_____ 7. –gen-: generate, generous, congenial

_____ 8. –able, -ible: remarkable, possible, probable

_____ 9. in-, im-, il-, ir-: intention, immerse, inspect

_____ 10. –scrib-, script- : manuscript, scribble, inscribe

f. capable of

g. in, into, on

h. write

i. birth, creation

j. state of being

6 Use the dictionary to find a word you don't know that uses the word part. Write the meaning of the word part, the word, and the definition. If your dictionary has the etymology (history) of the word, see how the word part relates to the meaning, and write the etymology after the definition.

Word Part	Meaning	Word	Definition and Etymology
EXAMPLE:			
ir-	not	irrefragable	incapable of being refuted or disproved
			Latin in-, not + refrāgārī, to oppose
1. clar-			
2. gen-			
3. il-			
4. in-			

5. *mal-* _____

_____

_____

_____

14 Fitness

A Healthy Body

Are you eating too much or exercising too little? Or both?

A Healthy Body

A healthy body isn't impossible to achieve. First you have to **confront** what is keeping you from being as healthy as you should be. Are you eating too much or exercising too little? Or both?   5

Getting in shape isn't a **fluke**; it takes hard work and **dedication**. But your workouts do not have to be **grueling** either. Find an activity you like to do and set up a workout **regimen**. Put your workouts on your calendar: walk Mon., Wed., and Fri. 9–10 A.M. Don't let a setback **fluster** you. If you forget to walk on Wednesday, don't give up. Walk on Friday and you will be fine.   10   15

Some people like activities that involve **opposition**. If you need to compete with someone pick a sport like tennis. Having people to play against can keep you training. Make your activity as **intense** as you can handle. People handle stress differently. Some people like to compete with others and some don't. Do what makes you happy, so you will keep doing it.   20   25

Also watch what you eat as part of your health regimen. Eat a balanced diet and eat in **moderation**. With a careful diet and steady exercise, you will **triumph** and have the body you desire.   30

Predicting

Circle the definition that best fits each vocabulary word. If you have difficulty, return to the reading on page 74, and underline any context clues you find. After you've made your predictions, check your answers against the Word List below. Place a checkmark in the boxes next to the words whose definitions you missed. These are the words you'll want to study closely.

NOTE: You may want to cover the Word List below with a piece of paper so you don't accidentally see the definitions as you do the Predicting exercise.

❑ 1. **confront** (line 3)
    a. to face head on
    b. to move behind
    c. to step aside

❑ 2. **fluke** (line 7)
    a. a lucky chance
    b. a musical instrument
    c. part of an elephant

❑ 3. **dedication** (line 8)
    a. state of being devoted
    b. act of being pained
    c. state of being careless

❑ 4. **grueling** (line 9)
    a. easy
    b. exhausting
    c. fighting

❑ 5. **regimen** (line 11)
    a. a king
    b. a practice area
    c. a plan

❑ 6. **fluster** (line 14)
    a. state of giving
    b. state of confusion
    c. act of staying calm

❑ 7. **opposition** (line 18)
    a. a game played with rackets
    b. a partner
    c. a contestant one is matched against

❑ 8. **intense** (line 21)
    a. lazy
    b. to an extreme degree
    c. automatic

❑ 9. **moderation** (line 28)
    a. having no control
    b. avoidance of extremes
    c. a new type of food

❑ 10. **triumph** (line 29)
    a. to win
    b. to lose
    c. to avoid

Word List

confront [kən frunt′]	*v.* to face head on		**grueling** [groo′ ə ling]	*adj.* tiring; exhausting
dedication [ded′ ə kā′ shən]	*n.* 1. the state of being devoted to a cause 2. a message attached to a book or other artistic work to show thanks or respect 3. a ceremony to open a building		**intense** [in tens′]	*adj.* to an extreme degree; deep
			moderation [mod′ ər ā′ shən]	*n.* avoidance of extremes; control
dedicate [ded′ ə kāt′]	*v.* to devote		**opposition** [äp′ ə zish′ ən]	*n.* 1. a contestant one is matched against 2. conflict; disagreement
fluke [flook]	*n.* a lucky chance; accidental good luck		**regimen** [rej′ ə mən, -men′]	*n.* a plan; discipline
fluster [flus′ tûr]	*n.* a state of confusion *v.* to upset; to cause confused behavior		**triumph** [trī′ əmpf]	*v.* to win; to overcome *n.* the joy of victory

Self-Tests

1 Put a T for true or F for false next to each sentence.

_____ 1. When confronted with a problem, it can be a good idea to think about it for awhile before making a decision.

_____ 2. Dedications in books are often addressed to parents or other family members.

_____ 3. Winning the lottery is a fluke.

_____ 4. Spending a relaxing day at home would fluster most people.

_____ 5. Climbing one of the highest mountains in the world would be grueling.

_____ 6. Writing a thousand-page book is an intense experience.

_____ 7. A parent and teenager agreeing on the time to come home from a date shows opposition.

_____ 8. Eating anything you want shows a strict dietary regimen.

_____ 9. Buying ten new outfits every day shows moderation in spending habits.

_____ 10. Finding a cure for cancer would be a triumph.

2 Finish these headlines using the vocabulary words. Use each word once.

Vocabulary List

confronts	dedicates	fluke	flustered	grueling
intense	opposition	regimen	moderation	triumphs

1. Huge Sports _____ : Against All Odds U.S. Wins the World Cup!

2. Tiger Woods Gets _____ ; Ends Up in the Sand Trap

3. Tour de France Update: Ten Riders Fade in _____ Mountain Stage

4. The _____ that Wins — Jordan's Training Secrets for Guaranteed Success

5. _____ Is the Key to Avoiding Burnout When Training for a Marathon

6. Wimbledon Veteran Faces Tough _____ from Newcomer

7. New Information on Steroid Use _____ **the NFL**

8. Pitcher _____ **His Talents to Youth Camp**

9. Gymnast _____ **: From Spinal Injury to Gold Medal**

10. _____ **Wind Delays Slalom Events**

3 In each group, circle the word that does not have a connection to the other three words.

1. upset	fluster	calm	confuse
2. discipline	uncontrolled	plan	regimen
3. intense	strong	extreme	weak
4. lucky	fluke	misfortune	accidental
5. refreshing	tiring	grueling	exhausting
6. opposition	cooperation	competition	disagreement
7. commit	dedicate	devote	avoid
8. mild	limit	extreme	moderation
9. retreat	face	confront	brave
10. triumph	lose	win	overcome

4 For each set, replace the underlined synonym or definition with the correct vocabulary word. Use each word once.

SET ONE

1. "I write down what I eat every day, and I go to the gym four days a week. I really feel healthier now that I am following this plan." _____

2. "We were down by two points and won just as the clock ran out. We deserved to win since we were able to overcome injuries and bad calls by the referees." _____

3. "Welcome to the opening of Lewiston Hall, which honors one of the first graduates of this university." _____

4. "What a lucky chance. You didn't study for the test and Professor Winston was absent. I heard that he hasn't missed a day in the last seven years." _____

5. "This dance step has me confused. Every time I try it I fall down." _____

Vocabulary List

flustered

dedication

fluke

triumph

regimen

Vocabulary List				
moderation	grueling	intense	opposition	confront

6. "The other contestants should be here soon, but I understand they won't be hard to beat." _____

7. "Don't force the stretch; control is the key to yoga. Try to avoid extremes." _____

8. "I need to face my problem: I am a chocoholic." _____

9. "This run is exhausting. It seems like we have been climbing hills all day." _____

10. "I don't like to play against him. His desire to win is too extreme; I just want to have fun." _____

Interactive Exercise

Answer the following questions as they apply to your life:

1. What have you shown dedication toward? _____

2. What most flusters you? _____

3. What was your most grueling experience you've had? _____

_____

4. What is the toughest opposition you've faced? _____

5. What is something you need to do in moderation? _____

6. What is the toughest problem you have confronted? _____

7. What has been the biggest fluke in your life? _____

8. What is the most intense experience you've had? _____

_____

9. What is the hardest regimen you've had to follow? _____

_____

10. What is your greatest triumph? _____

_____

A Healthy Wallet

FIRST MUTUAL

September 10, 2004

Dear Investor,

In these **uncertain** times we are all looking for a safe place to put our money and that is why First Mutual is
holding a special **seminar** entitled "Your Money Today and Tomorrow." The seminar will feature a day of   5
discussion on investing in the stock market, certificates of deposit, and other ways to **diversify** your financial
holdings. The only way to **acquire** peace of mind for your future is to **invest** your money wisely today.
With the right **attitude** people can learn how to make their money work for them.

Many people have **overextended** themselves and the seminar will also include meetings on debt
management. Our advisors will **prescribe** several remedies for your financial troubles. Don't **compound**   10
your financial problems by avoiding them.

The seminar will be held Saturday, October 17 from 9– 4, lunch will be provided. Please call (555) 362-1504
today to reserve your spot. Don't put your future in a **precarious** position; know that your money is safe
with sound investments. First Mutual is here to help.

Sincerely,   15

Laura Griffin
Laura Griffin
VP Customer Services

Predicting

Circle the definition that best fits each vocabulary word. If you have difficulty, return to the reading on page 79, and underline any context clues you find. After you've made your predictions, check your answers against the Word List below. Place a checkmark in the boxes next to the words whose definitions you missed. These are the words you'll want to study closely.

NOTE: You may want to cover the Word List below with a piece of paper so you don't accidentally see the definitions as you do the Predicting exercise.

☐ 1. **uncertain** (line 4)
   a. doubtful
   b. positive
   c. careful

☐ 2. **seminar** (line 5)
   a. a large building
   b. a type of pasta
   c. a meeting or class

☐ 3. **diversify** (line 6)
   a. to keep the same
   b. to add variety
   c. to find out

☐ 4. **acquire** (line 7)
   a. to misplace
   b. to get possession of
   c. to sing

☐ 5. **invest** (line 7)
   a. to use something for profit
   b. to discourage a person
   c. to write a letter

☐ 6. **attitude** (line 8)
   a. way of thinking
   b. a type of money
   c. way of writing

☐ 7. **overextended** (line 9)
   a. tried to do too much
   b. wanted to leave
   c. moved too late

☐ 8. **prescribe** (line 10)
   a. to give as a guide
   b. to take a trip
   c. to hurt someone's feelings

☐ 9. **compound** (line 10)
   a. to decorate
   b. to increase
   c. to decrease

☐ 10. **precarious** (line 13)
   a. insecure
   b. safe
   c. final

Word List

acquire [ə kwīr′]	*v.* to get possession of	
attitude [at′ ə tōōd′]	*n.* a way of thinking or behaving	
compound [kom′ pound] [kəm pound′]	*v.* to increase; to add to *adj.* combined *n.* a mixture of two or more things	
diversify [di vûr′ sə fī′]	*v.* to add variety; to vary; to expand	
invest [in vest′]	*v.* to use something for profit (ex. money, time)	

overextend [ō′ vûr ik stend′]	*v.* to promise more (money, time, etc.) than one can deliver; to try to do too much
precarious [pri kâr′ ē əs]	*adj.* 1. insecure; dangerously lacking security 2. subject to change
prescribe [pri skrīb′]	*v.* to give as a rule or guide; to recommend the use of
seminar [sem′ ə när′]	*n.* a meeting or class for discussion of a particular subject
uncertain [un′ sûrt′ n]	*adj.* not known; doubtful; undecided

Self-Tests

I Match the word to its definition.

_____ 1. prescribe   a. to use something for profit

_____ 2. diversify   b. a meeting or class

_____ 3. seminar   c. to recommend the use of

_____ 4. uncertain   d. to get possession of

_____ 5. precarious   e. a way of thinking

_____ 6. invest   f. not known

_____ 7. acquire   g. a mixture of two or more things

_____ 8. overextend   h. subject to change

_____ 9. attitude   i. to add variety

_____ 10. compound   j. to promise more than one can deliver

2 Finish the analogies. See the Analogies Appendix on page 143 for instructions and practice.

Vocabulary List

| prescribes | diversify | acquire | attitude | overextend |
| precarious | uncertain | seminar | invest | compound |

1. hungry : full :: sure : _____

2. eat : a meal : : _____ : knowledge

3. deadline : work late :: _____ : frustration

4. end : finish :: _____ : meeting

5. red : rose :: positive : _____

6. chef : cooks :: doctor : _____

7. tall : big :: add to : _____

8. devote : energy : : _____ : time

9. simple : elaborate :: unify : _____

10. stealing a purse : villainous :: standing on the edge of a cliff : _____

3 For Set One match each term with its synonym. For Set Two match each term with its antonym.

SYNONYMS
SET ONE

_____   1. attitude   a. vary

_____   2. seminar   b. doubtful

_____   3. diversify   c. view

_____   4. prescribe   d. meeting

_____   5. uncertain   e. suggest

ANTONYMS
SET TWO

_____   6. overextend   f. secure

_____   7. acquire   g. conserve

_____   8. compound   h. waste

_____   9. precarious   i. give

_____   10. invest   j. decrease

4 Finish the reading using the vocabulary words. Use each word once.

Vocabulary List				
acquiring	compounded	overextended	uncertain	diversify
seminar	prescribed	investing	precarious	attitude

My financial situation is (1)_____ right now because I'm almost bankrupt. I spent way more over the past seven months than I make. I'm about to lose everything that I have.

It seems like I will never learn. Even last month I (2)_____ again when I charged $1,200 on my credit card for an engagement ring for my girlfriend. I also spend $700 on rent and $400 on my car payment, plus other bills. My (3)_____ about money has changed from enjoying it to fearing debt. I actually used to think about (4)_____ in stocks for my future; now I worry about how I'm ever going to get caught up with my payments.

Last week I attended a financial planning (5)_____. At this class, financial planners discussed ways of changing one's financial situation. They suggested I write down every penny I spend, and then evaluate my own spending habits. They said that most people concentrate on (6)_____ more money, rather than considering how they actually spend the money they already have. I thought the seminar would be more complex. I expected to learn about how to (7)_____ my investments in stocks, bonds, and other areas. I thought I would learn how interest is (8)_____. Instead they (9)_____ practical solutions using the money I already have. There are things in my life I am (10)_____ about, but I am sure I can make my financial life healthy again.

Interactive Exercise

Write two responses for each of the following topics.

1. What are you uncertain about?

   1. _____   2. _____

2. What are you most interested in acquiring in life?

   1. _____   2. _____

3. What are some attitudes people have towards money?

   1. _____   2. _____

4. What activities would you prescribe for someone who is depressed?

   1. _____   2. _____

5. How do people overextend themselves?

   1. _____   2. _____

6. What do people invest in (besides stocks and bonds)?

   1. _____   2. _____

7. What would a precarious situation be?

   1. _____   2. _____

8. What type of seminar would you like to attend?

   1. _____   2. _____

9. What are ways to compound a problem?

   1. _____   2. _____

10. How would you like to diversify your interests?

   1. _____   2. _____

A Healthy Environment

June 25

It is the second night of my environmental awareness retreat. We have been camped out in the forest to learn how the world is changing. I didn't know what to **anticipate** when I signed up. I hoped it wasn't going to be a **dismal** weekend of complaining about how badly humans are treating the planet. And it hasn't been. There is hope for the Earth! The instructors have been great in showing us what we can do from following **trends** such as recycling to writing key officials in Washington to **stimulate** their interest in environmental legislation. If we want to save the planet, we must not be **impassive.** Some of the damage isn't **irrevocable.** With the right efforts we can clean up contaminated streams and save endangered animals. I can't wait for tomorrow's activities.

5

10

June 26

Today the instructors focused on how environmental issues are **global** concerns. For example, the **depletion** of the ozone layer is a worldwide problem, and the loss of protection that layer supplies may lead to health difficulties everywhere. I am an **avid** fan of nature, and I want to help keep the planet beautiful. It has been so peaceful here in the forest; I don't want places like this to disappear. What I learned most is that if we all **cooperate,** we can have a healthy environment! All we need to do is work together.

15

Predicting

Circle the definition that best fits each vocabulary word. If you have difficulty, return to the reading on page 84, and underline any context clues you find. After you've made your predictions, check your answers against the Word List below. Place a checkmark in the boxes next to the words whose definitions you missed. These are the words you'll want to study closely.

NOTE: You may want to cover the Word List below with a piece of paper so you don't accidentally see the definitions as you do the Predicting exercise.

☐ 1. **anticipate** (line 4)
   a. to fear
   b. to join in
   c. to expect

☐ 2. **dismal** (line 4)
   a. miserable
   b. wonderful
   c. short

☐ 3. **trend** (line 7)
   a. a form
   b. a general direction
   c. a dependable person

☐ 4. **stimulate** (line 8)
   a. to excite
   b. to bore
   c. to hurt

☐ 5. **impassive** (line 9)
   a. excited
   b. having a lack of interest
   c. worried

☐ 6. **irrevocable** (line 9)
   a. unchangeable
   b. changeable
   c. hurt

☐ 7. **global** (line 13)
   a. bright
   b. healthy
   c. international

☐ 8. **depletion** (line 14)
   a. increase
   b. reduction
   c. abundance

☐ 9. **avid** (line 16)
   a. depressed
   b. enthusiastic
   c. foaming

☐ 10. **cooperate** (line 18)
   a. to work together
   b. to disagree
   c. to remove

Word List

anticipate [an tis′ ə pāt′]	*v.*	to look forward to; to expect	**global** [glō′ bəl]	*adj.*	involving the entire Earth; international
avid [av′ id]	*adj.*	eager; enthusiastic	**impassive** [im pas′ iv]	*adj.*	having a lack of interest; not showing emotion; expressionless
cooperate [kō äp′ ər āt]	*v.*	to work together; to agree	**irrevocable** [i rev′ ə kə bəl]	*adj.*	unchangeable; final; permanent
depletion [di plē′ shən]	*n.*	the act of decreasing something; reduction	**stimulate** [stim′ yə lāt′]	*v.*	to excite; to inspire; to cause to do
dismal [diz′ məl]	*adj.*	miserable; depressing; dull	**trend** [trend]	*n.*	a general direction in which something tends to move; a leaning

Self-Tests

1

Finish the sentences using the vocabulary words below. Use each word once.

1. I don't like to follow the latest fashion _____, but my sister does. She reads several fashion magazines.

2. My dad is a(n) _____ reader of mysteries; he has over two thousand mystery books.

3. My brother's day was _____ after he got two flat tires on his bike.

4. Taking a trip around the world would be a _____ experience.

5. There has been a rapid _____ of snacks in the kitchen since Anthony got home from college.

6. Cheering someone on in a race can _____ the person to do better.

7. My nephew is eagerly _____ his birthday; he can't wait to see if he will get the race car set he asked for.

8. My neighbor is _____; he never joins in any of the activities we have on the block.

9. Cleaning the house together shows _____.

10. My instructor said my grade was _____; there was nothing I could do to change it.

Vocabulary List

anticipating

avid

trends

impassive

stimulate

global

cooperation

dismal

irrevocable

depletion

2

Put a T for true or F for false next to each statement.

_____ 1. A lot of people are avid about sports.

_____ 2. A politician tries to stimulate interest in his or her campaign.

_____ 3. Cell phones are a fast-growing trend.

_____ 4. Most people consider a sunny day dismal.

_____ 5. People can set up a will that is irrevocable.

_____ 6. There has been a depletion of the Earth's overall population in the last two hundred years.

_____ 7. At the airport most people anticipate some sort of delay.

_____ 8. If a child refuses to help pick up his toys, he shows he knows how to cooperate.

_____ 9. Walking to my neighborhood park is an example of a global activity.

_____ 10. Shouting for one's favorite team to win and crying when they lose would be the actions of an impassive person.

3 Circle the word that best completes the sentence.

1. I am disappointed in the (global, dismal) turnout for the meeting; I guess the bad weather scared people away.

2. To (stimulate, cooperate) interest in the upcoming concert, the band marched around campus during the lunch hour for a week.

3. I am an (irrevocable, avid) bicyclist; I ride at least thirty miles every day.

4. The (global, avid) meeting on how to achieve worldwide peace will be held in Berlin this May with over two hundred countries represented.

5. There has been a (depletion, trend) in our water supply because we had so little rain this year.

6. We (cooperate, anticipate) a full house at the meeting; the water conservation issue has upset a lot of people.

7. The committee assignments are (impassive, irrevocable). We can't have people constantly moving from one place to another; you must stay on your committee until the job is done.

8. I wonder what the latest fashion (trend, depletion) will be; I hope it isn't silly like platform shoes.

9. Because everyone was able to (anticipate, cooperate), the project was completed a month ahead of schedule.

10. The public has become so (impassive, avid) that almost no one votes anymore.

4 Finish the story by using the words to the right. Use each word once.

Keri wanted to stop being (1)_____ and start helping the environment. She decided to begin with her neighborhood. She didn't want people to see the situation as being (2)_____. She wanted to show that environmental problems are not (3)_____; she wanted to show her neighbors that people can change the world. Keri decided that to (4)_____ an interest in environmental issues she would have an Environmental Fair with food, games, and information booths at the neighborhood park. She knew there were some (5)_____ environmentalists in her neighborhood like Dan. Dan recycled everything, drove an electric car, and joined protests to save endangered animals. Keri went to Dan's house to discuss the Fair.

"Keri, have you (6)_____ all the problems you will have putting on this event?"

"I know it won't be easy, but since it will benefit the Earth, I am willing to work hard. I also know there are people who will (7)_____ with me in organizing this event—like you."

"Okay, Keri, you have my participation. Let's think (8)_____ and then narrow down our ideas to the neighborhood. We can have a display on the (9)_____ of resources worldwide and then show our neighbors how they can help to save those resources."

Vocabulary List

dismal

avid

irrevocable

depletion

impassive

trends

cooperate

stimulate

globally

anticipated

"One of the (10)_____ that I want to support is recycling, with bins for paper, plastic, and cans all over the park. Maybe the bins can even stay after the Fair."

"That's a great idea. I have some thoughts on the food we can offer and fun environmental games. Let's sit down and start planning. I am proud of you, Keri, for taking this on!"

Interactive Exercise

Below is a chapter from an imaginary textbook about the environment. Complete the exercises to gain practice in using the vocabulary words.

The Environment and You

Lesson 1

What do you know about the environment? Test your environmental awareness by answering the following questions. These matters will be discussed in the rest of the text.

Exercise I. List two *global* environmental problems.
Example: *depletion* of forests worldwide

1. _____ 2. _____

Exercise II. What do you consider the most *dismal* situation involving the environment? Do you think it is *irrevocable?*

_____

_____

Exercise III. List two ways you can *stimulate* people to become *avid* environmentalists. Think about current *trends,* such as recycling, to develop your list.

1. _____ 2. _____

People are often *impassive,* and it can be hard to get them to *cooperate.* List two problems you would *anticipate* in getting people involved.

1. _____ 2. _____

17 Review

Focus on Chapters 9–16

For instructions, see page 90.

1. _____

2. _____

3. _____

4. _____

5. _____

6. _____

7. _____

8. _____

9. _____

10. _____

11. _____

12. _____

The following activities give you a chance to interact some more with the vocabulary words you've been learning. By looking at art, acting, writing, taking tests, and doing a crossword puzzle, you will see which words you know well and which you still need to work with.

Art

Match each picture on page 89 to one of the following vocabulary words. Use each word once.

Vocabulary List

depletion	gallery	novice	sequence
opposition	attitude	revelation	monotonous
superlative	burden	triumph	villainous

Collaborative Activity: Drama

Charades: You will be given one of the following words to act out in class. Think about how this word could be demonstrated without speaking. The other people in class will try to guess what word you are showing.

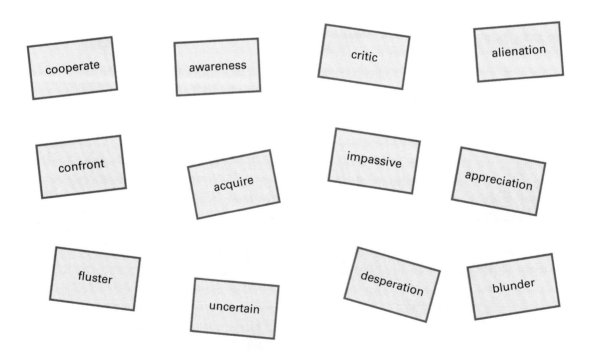

cooperate

awareness

critic

alienation

confront

acquire

impassive

appreciation

fluster

uncertain

desperation

blunder

Writing

Answer the following questions to further test your understanding of the vocabulary words.

1. What are two trends that you think have been silly? _____

_____

2. Pick a holiday and list two items that symbolize it. _____

_____

3. List one of the preliminary steps for preparing to go to college. _____

_____

4. What sport are you avid about? Or whom do you know who is an avid sports fan?

_____

5. What activity do you consider grueling? _____

6. What kind of seminar would you like to lead someday? _____

_____

7. What event would you like to read the chronicles of? _____

8. What kind of buff are you? _____

9. List an event or activity that you would consider a fluke. _____

_____

10. What would you prescribe someone do to relieve stress? _____

_____

HINT

Use It or Lose It

When you learn a new word, you must take an important step before the word is actually a part of *your* vocabulary: Use it outside the classroom. When you feel that you understand the word, you must use it—not once but as often as you can. If you continue to use it—even if you don't feel comfortable doing so at first—the word will become part of your active vocabulary. *It will belong to you.* Learning vocabulary is all about using words, not about memorizing definitions. If you know the definition of a word but can't use it when you are speaking or writing, what good is it to you?

Self-Tests

1 Finish the reading using the vocabulary words below. Use each word once.

Vocabulary List

associated	categories	dedication	contention	elaborate
generate	invest	qualify	sufficient	relevance

BIG PLANS

The meeting on what to do for the (1)_____ of the college's new Inspiration Garden really got crazy. The garden was built as a place where students could sit and think in peaceful surroundings. The plans for the opening started to get (2)_____. People wanted to bring in dancers and rock bands and offer food from local restaurants. There was even the suggestion of a dance contest and the finalists would (3)_____ for a drawing for a reserved parking space for the semester. Someone finally said that we didn't have (4)_____ funds to put on such a complicated event. Someone suggested we could (5)_____ the money through donations. Someone else mentioned that no one had the time to (6)_____ in getting the money. Then there was the (7)_____ that such a gathering didn't fit in with the quiet atmosphere of the garden. Finally, everyone agreed that the opening should have some (8)_____ to the purpose of the garden. We decided to put the ideas we thought were important into a few (9)_____ and focus on those items. By the end of the meeting we had planned a simple, but meaningful event. I was proud to be (10)_____ with the planning committee.

2 Pick the word that best completes each sentence.

1. I didn't _____ my homework taking so long. Now I don't know if I will finish.

   a. acquire   b. anticipate   c. generate   d. cooperate

2. I hate it when a movie gets a lot of _____. A movie usually can't live up to my expectations when so much has been said about it.

   a. revelation   b. attitude   c. contention   d. hype

3. I enjoy _____ that has the main character battling with nature.

   a. triumph   b. seminar   c. fiction   d.   novice

4. My brother is a _____; he is always dreaming up impractical inventions.

   a. visionary   b. gallery   c. burden   d.   fluke

5. I am angry at Marsha for putting me in such a _____. She was supposed to meet my train and she isn't here, and now I don't know what to do.

   a. category   b. predicament   c. sequence   d.   depletion

6. Judy thought cleaning up after her son was _____ since his room was dirty the next day.

   a. superfluous   b. maladjusted   c. global   d.   futile

7. Mom's first marriage came as a _____ to Dad when he got a call from her ex-husband.

   a. blunder   b. chronicle   c. revelation   c.   dedication

8. Dennis found skydiving to be an _____ experience; it was extremely exciting.

   a. uncertain   b. intense   c. avid   d.   elaborate

9. There is _____ interest in an English Club. Fifty people showed up for the first meeting.

   a. sufficiently   b. elaborately   c. critically   d.   obviously

10. I don't _____ easily, but when I couldn't find my research paper, I got upset.

   a. fluster   b. overextend   c. cooperate   d.   jeopardize

Crossword Puzzle

Vocabulary List

abstract

absurdity

associated

clarity

compound

contrived

dismal

diversify

global

irrevocable

jeopardize

maladjusted

manuscript

moderation

novice

overextend

precarious

regimen

stimulate

superfluous

Across

5. avoidance of extremes
6. more than is needed
8. fake
13. a plan; discipline
15. to try to do too much
17. clearness
19. to excite
20. nonsense

Down

1. to add variety
2. to threaten
3. complex
4. emotionally unstable
7. related to
9. final
10. to add to
11. a written document
12. subject to change
14. a beginner
16. international
18. depressing

18 Personalities

As the Cookie Crumbles

How do we know who we are? What the future holds? The answer is simple: we have only to open a fortune cookie to find our true personalities. Do any of these fortunes sound like you?

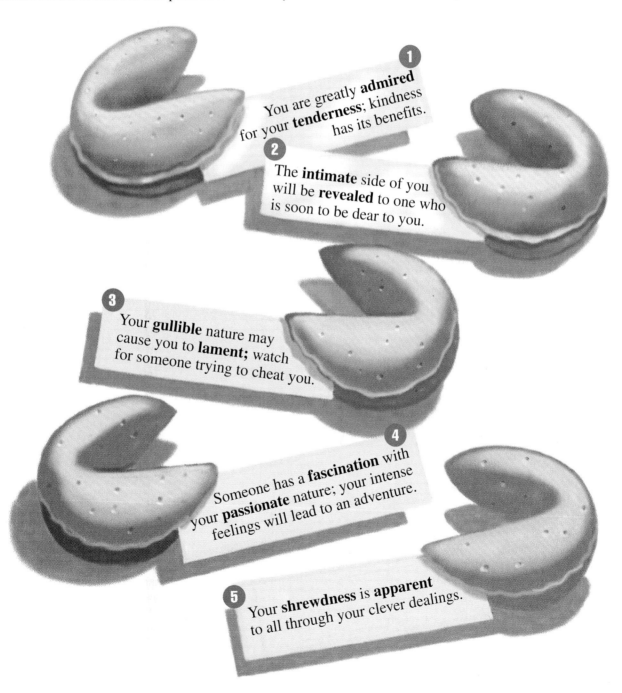

1 You are greatly **admired** for your **tenderness**; kindness has its benefits.

2 The **intimate** side of you will be **revealed** to one who is soon to be dear to you.

3 Your **gullible** nature may cause you to **lament**; watch for someone trying to cheat you.

4 Someone has a **fascination** with your **passionate** nature; your intense feelings will lead to an adventure.

5 Your **shrewdness** is **apparent** to all through your clever dealings.

Predicting

Circle the definition that best fits each vocabulary word. If you have difficulty, return to the reading on page 95, and underline any context clues you find. After you've made your predictions, check your answers against the Word List below. Place a checkmark in the boxes next to the words whose definitions you missed. These are the words you'll want to study closely.

NOTE: You may want to cover the Word List below with a piece of paper so you don't accidentally see the definitions as you do the Predicting exercise.

❑ 1. **admire** (fortune 1)
   a. to cry
   b. to think highly of
   c. to get stuck in the mud

❑ 2. **tenderness** (fortune 1)
   a. abandonment
   b. cruelty
   c. warm feelings

❑ 3. **intimate** (fortune 2)
   a. stubborn
   b. formal
   c. of a personal nature

❑ 4. **reveal** (fortune 2)
   a. to stop doing
   b. to party
   c. to display

❑ 5. **gullible** (fortune 3)
   a. very fast
   b. easily fooled
   c. smoothly said

❑ 6. **lament** (fortune 3)
   a. to express grief
   b. to pour concrete
   c. to come near

❑ 7. **fascination** (fortune 4)
   a. extreme interest
   b. a hook
   c. mismanagement

❑ 8. **passionate** (fortune 4)
   a. old
   b. enthusiastic
   c. bored

❑ 9. **shrewdness** (fortune 5)
   a. freedom
   b. a small animal
   c. intelligence

❑ 10. **apparent** (fortune 5)
   a. courageous
   b. clear
   c. confusing

Word List

admire [ad mīər']	v.	to think highly of; respect	**lament** [lə ment']	v. to express grief
apparent [ə par' ənt, ə pâr'-]	adj.	easily seen or understood; clear; evident	**passionate** [pash' ən it]	adj. having strong emotions; enthusiastic; loving
fascination [fas' ə nā' shən]	n.	extreme interest; enchantment	**reveal** [ri vēl']	v. to make known; to display
gullible [gul' ə bəl]	adj.	easily fooled; believing	**shrewdness** [shro͞od' nis]	n. intelligence; common sense
intimate [in' tə mit]	adj.	of a close, personal, or private nature	**tenderness** [ten' dər nes]	n. warm feelings; softness

Self-Tests

1 Match the vocabulary word to the situation it best fits. Use the underlined context clues to help you make the connections. Context clues may be synonyms, antonyms, examples, or the general meaning of a sentence.

SET ONE

_____ 1. Elaine is grieving over her hamster's death.

_____ 2. Steve's brother knocked on the door and ran away six times; his brother got up to answer it every time.

_____ 3. Because Suzy is her close friend, Leslie shared a family secret with her.

_____ 4. The little boy is extremely interested in building; he plays with his blocks for hours.

_____ 5. Stacey put her arm around her nervous little sister as they entered school the first day.

a. gullible

b. lament

c. tenderness

d. intimate

e. fascination

SET TWO

_____ 6. The man turned a $50 investment into $5,000.

_____ 7. When the monster took off his mask, we were surprised to discover Jim.

_____ 8. The math major was enthusiastic about his homework. He stayed up all night solving equations, and he wanted more.

_____ 9. Barney shook his teacher's hand at the end of the semester and told her how much he respected her.

_____ 10. Mom and Dad came home and saw the pile of paper plates in the trash and the soda stains on the rug; it was clear there had been a party.

f. reveal

g. admire

h. apparent

i. passionate

j. shrewdness

2 Complete the sentences using the word list below. Use each word once.

Vocabulary List				
admire	tenderness	intimate	reveal	lamented
gullible	fascination	passionate	shrewdness	apparent

1. Teachers _____ students who study hard. They regard these students highly because they see the pride the students feel for themselves.

2. It is _____ that you like to eat Chinese food; you have gone to four Chinese restaurants this week.

3. A _____ student will be enthusiastic about studying.

4. She shared the most _____ details of her love life with her best friend.

5. The student showed his _____ when he took the time to study instead of going to the party.

6. He was afraid to _____ his true feelings about loving to cook because his father thought it was something only women did.

7. After he failed the test, the student _____ going to the party instead of studying.

8. My _____ with the stars led me to take an astronomy class.

9. Because of the student's _____ nature, he believed the teacher when she said, "I like it when students come to class unprepared." The next day he felt foolish when he didn't bring his textbook.

10. The mother's _____ toward her baby was easy to see when she hugged him.

3 In each group, circle the word that does not have a connection to the other three words.

1. warmth   softness   cruelty   tenderness

2. grieve   laugh ·   lament   cry

3. confused   clear   apparent   plain

4. excited   passionate   bored   enthusiastic

5. believing   trustful   gullible   suspicious

6. hate   respect   admire   love

7. intimate   private   close   public

8. wisdom   intelligence   stupidity   shrewdness

9. attraction   fascination   enchantment   loathing

10. reveal   hide   show   display

4 For each set, answer the questions about the quotations. Look for context clues to help you. Use each word once.

SET ONE

1. "My sister, Daphne, was able to turn a run-down restaurant into a gourmet café. I admire her financial skills." What kind of intelligence does Daphne have? _____

2. "I write my private thoughts in a diary." What kind of thoughts does the person write?
_____

3. "Carlos is enthusiastic about cooking spicy food; he loves to make hot dishes." How does Carlos feel about cooking? _____

4. "Anyone could easily see that their marriage wasn't going to last; they had nothing in common." How obvious was it to people that the marriage was going to fail? _____

5. "In just a moment I will display the statue I have spent the last year creating." What is the artist going to do to the statue? _____

SET TWO

Vocabulary List				
lament	admire	tenderness	gullible	fascination

6. "I am miserable today. My dog died last night, and I've had him since I was eight." What is the person going to do about the dog's death? _____

7. "Petula enjoys watching her fish for hours. She says their movements are 'enchanting.'" What does Petula feel for her fish? _____

8. "Freddie works hard for the community, and they think highly of him. They held a dinner last night to honor him." How does the community feel about Freddie? _____

9. "Let me give you a hug; you really have had a hard day." What is the person showing? _____

10. "I can't believe I wore my pajamas to the party. I didn't realize you were joking when you said to. Why am I so easy to fool?" What kind of person is the speaker? _____

Interactive Exercise

Imagine that you write fortunes for cookies. Using the vocabulary words on page 96, complete the first fortunes, and then write two of your own.

Your _____ toward a friend will _____ a surprising secret.

Your _____ with the stars will lead to a _____ affair.

People _____ your _____ you for _____ in business.

19 Friendship

Thank You for Everything

Dear Lee,

Thank you for the lovely house-warming gift. The rug is exquisite; it is a perfect match for my couch. I also want to thank you for being so **supportive** over the years. You have kept my secrets **confidential** and given your **sympathy** when I have been upset. You are a person whose **advice** I can trust. What you suggest I do almost always works out. I like to **assume** that I have been a good friend too. I hope I have not **neglected** you these last few months while I have been busy purchasing the house.

Unfortunately, we have had to put up with some **malicious** people over the years (remember Terri from high school—she really tried to destroy our friendship), but we have come through it all. We learned how to **compromise** on that car trip across the United States. I don't regret turning down my music at night so you could get to sleep, and I thank you for letting me stop at every tacky tourist shop even though that wasn't your favorite activity. Over the years we have really had the chance to **empathize** with each other as we have faced romantic setbacks, family disasters, and personal problems. I appreciate your going through everything with me. If there was ever a **rift** in our relationship, I don't know what I would do.

Now that I'm settled, I want you to visit often. Can you make it for dinner next week? I'll call you!

Thanks,
Pat

5

10

15

20

25

Predicting

Circle the definition that best fits each vocabulary word. If you have difficulty, return to the reading on page 100, and underline any context clues you find. After you've made your predictions, check your answers against the Word List below. Place a checkmark in the boxes next to the words whose definitions you missed. These are the words you'll want to study closely.

NOTE: You may want to cover the Word List below with a piece of paper so you don't accidentally see the definitions as you do the Predicting exercise.

☐ 1. **supportive** (line 4)
   a. fun
   b. helpful
   c. mean

☐ 2. **confidential** (line 5)
   a. public
   b. secret
   c. serious

☐ 3. **sympathy** (line 5)
   a. a feeling of tenderness
   b. a display of anger
   c. madness

☐ 4. **advice** (line 6)
   a. an order
   b. an opinion on how to act
   c. an old friend

☐ 5. **assume** (line 7)
   a. to know
   b. to be relieved
   c. to believe

☐ 6. **neglected** (line 8)
   a. spoke with
   b. overlooked
   c. worried about

☐ 7. **malicious** (line 11)
   a. showing a desire to harm another
   b. wanting to do good
   c. filled with delight

☐ 8. **compromise** (line 14)
   a. to play loud music
   b. to disagree
   c. to settle a difference by working together

☐ 9. **empathize** (line 19)
   a. to misunderstand what someone says
   b. to understand a person's feelings
   c. to search for a better way

☐ 10. **rift** (line 21)
   a. a break
   b. a wave
   c. a bond

Word List

advice [ad vīs′]	*n.* an opinion on how to act; a recommendation		**malicious** [mə lish′ əs]	*adj.* feeling or showing a desire to harm another; hateful; mean
assume [ə soom′]	*v.* 1. to suppose; to believe 2. to take on		**neglect** [ni glekt′]	*v.* to overlook; to fail to pay attention to
compromise [kom′ prə mīz]	*v.* to settle a difference by working together and modifying one's demands		**rift** [rift]	*n.* a break; division; split
confidential [kän′ fə den′ chəl]	*adj.* spoken or written for only a few people to know about; secret		**supportive** [sə pôr′ tiv]	*adj.* giving strength and encouragement; helpful
empathize [em′ pə thīz]	*v.* to identify with another person's situation; to understand a person's feelings		**sympathy** [sim′ pə thē]	*n.* 1. a feeling of tenderness or sorrow for another person's pain 2. a feeling of loyalty

Self-Tests

1 For each set, match the sentence to the kind of comment it best demonstrates. Use each type once.

SET ONE

Kind of comment

giving empathy	poor advice	malicious	supportive	assuming something

1. "Oh, I had always believed Joan was married." _____

2. "I'm sorry to hear about your father's death. I understand how you feel; my father passed away last month." _____

3. "I recommend that you don't do any work for a week; then maybe they'll appreciate you!" _____

4. "Joe is always so perfect. I can't take it anymore. The boss is going to have to hear something bad about him." _____

5. "You'll be great at the concert; you're an excellent pianist." _____

SET TWO

Kind of comment

confidential	giving sympathy	could lead to neglect	could cause a rift	suggesting a compromise

6. "I'm sorry everyone laughed at you when you asked that question. I didn't think it was dumb." _____

7. "There are several sporting events I want to watch on television, so I might not be able to pay much attention to you this weekend." _____

8. "I'll get up first in the morning to take a shower if you turn down the volume on the television at night." _____

9. "I'm going to quit this job, but it's still a secret, so don't tell anyone!" _____

10. "Tanya and Leo are fighting again. Their relationship is in trouble. I'm not trying to split them up, but I'll let his ex-girlfriend know because I heard she wants to get back together with him." _____

2 For Set One match each word with its synonym. For Set Two match each word with its antonym.

SYNONYMS
SET ONE

_____ 1. compromise   a. believe

_____ 2. rift   b. adjust

_____ 3. advice   c. identify

_____ 4. empathize   d. split

_____ 5. assume   e. suggestion

ANTONYMS

SET TWO

_____ 6. malicious   f. open

_____ 7. confidential   g. care

_____ 8. supportive   h. cruelty

_____ 9. neglect   i. kind

_____ 10. sympathy   j. discouraging

3 Use the vocabulary words to complete the following analogies. For instructions on how to complete analogies, see the Analogies Appendix on page 143.

Vocabulary List

compromise	neglect	rift	sympathy	malicious
assume	confidential	advice	supportive	empathize

1. cold : hot :: union : _____

2. strong wind : downed power lines :: _____ : overgrown garden

3. contact : touch ::loyalty : _____

4. snow : white :: a code : _____

5. write : a form:: _____ : more responsibilities at work

6. angry : slow waiter :: _____ : a friend running for office

7. open a book : read :: meet a friend also going through a divorce : _____

8. simple : complex :: disagree : _____

9. taxi driver : ride :: counselor : _____

10. bashful : shy :: mean : _____

4 Circle the word that best completes each sentence.

1. I will (assume, neglect) office as president of the club in January.

2. The (advice, rift) in our friendship occurred over a silly disagreement.

3. The letter was supposed to be (malicious, confidential), but somehow everyone in the office found out about its contents.

4. I didn't (neglect, empathize) my studies because I wanted to do well in the class.

5. I listened to the instructor's (sympathy, advice) and studied every night.

6. I thought Pearl liked Wanda, but she made some (malicious, supportive) comments about her at lunch today.

7. By learning to (assume, compromise) my husband and I have enjoyed thirty years of marriage.

8. I showed my (rift, sympathy) for Jane's lost dog by sending her a card.

9. My coach has been especially (confidential, supportive) this semester; she has helped me through several personal problems.

10. I (empathize, compromise) with Alicia; I too had a hard time adjusting to college.

Interactive Exercise

Pretend you are Lee and write Pat back. Use at least seven vocabulary words in your response.

Dear Pat,

_____

_____

_____

_____

_____

_____

_____

_____

_____

_____

_____

_____

_____

_____

_____

_____

_____

_____

_____

Sincerely,

_____

20 Romance

The Flirting Seminar

Thank you all for coming this evening. My name is Emma Mansfield. Look around and you'll see men and women of all ages and backgrounds. Some of you are divorced, others are widowed, and others never married. But you all have something in common. You want to find a better way to **relate** to other people. First of all, I want to **clarify** something: there is nothing wrong with a little flirting. Some of you may think flirting will make you look pushy or **manipulative.** But flirting is a harmless way to get to know other people. It doesn't cost a thing, you can do it anywhere and any time, and it's fun!

Let's take an example. On a normal day you will complete simple tasks at the grocery, the post office, and so on. In each of these places, you have the opportunity to interact with people. What better way to practice the flirting techniques I'm going to give you? The rest of the evening I'm going to **disclose** the secrets behind successful flirting.

Look at the screen for a few basics to begin with.

1. Dress to **impress.** Always look your best. You never know who you'll run into.

2. **Establish** eye contact. Get the person to look at you. And smile.

3. Show **genuine** interest. Let him or her know that you're really interested.

You see, you never know when or where you're going to meet someone that you find attractive. If you make these techniques part of your everyday life, you'll be ready to enter the **uncharted** world of romance. People never know what they will find! If you pay close attention to the rest of the seminar I can **ensure** that you won't feel **intimidated;** you will be able to flirt with confidence in the future.

Predicting

Circle the definition that best fits each vocabulary word. If you have difficulty, return to the reading on page 105, and underline any context clues you find. After you've made your predictions, check your answers against the Word List below. Place a checkmark in the boxes next to the words whose definitions you missed. These are the words you'll want to study closely.

NOTE: You may want to cover the Word List below with a piece of paper so you don't accidentally see the definitions as you do the Predicting exercise.

☐ 1. **relate** (line 8)
    a. to connect
    b. to enjoy
    c. to play

☐ 2. **clarify** (line 9)
    a. to hurry
    b. to make clear
    c. to confuse

☐ 3. **manipulative** (line 13)
    a. controlling
    b. artistic
    c. carefree

☐ 4. **disclose** (line 21)
    a. to move aside
    b. to tell in private
    c. to make public

☐ 5. **impress** (line 24)
    a. to interest
    b. to work well
    c. to help

☐ 6. **establish** (line 26)
    a. to express
    b. to stop
    c. to form

☐ 7. **genuine** (line 27)
    a. real
    b. incredible
    c. funny

☐ 8. **uncharted** (line 30)
    a. unleashed
    b. unexplored
    c. mapped

☐ 9. **ensure** (line 32)
    a. to make certain
    b. to make one happy
    c. to make quiet

☐ 10. **intimidated** (line 32)
    a. ugly
    b. scared
    c. sorry

Word List

clarify [klâr′ ə fī]	*v.* to make clear; to explain	**impress** [im pres′]	*v.* to influence; to interest
disclose [dis klōz′]	*v.* to make public	**intimidated** [in tim′ i dā təd]	*adj.* scared; frightened
ensure [en shûr′] [en shoor′]	*v.* to make certain	**manipulative** [mə nip′ yə lā′ tiv] [mə nip′ yə lə tiv]	*adj.* using for one's own purposes; controlling
establish [e stab′ lish]	*v.* to form; to make	**relate** [rē lāt′]	*v.* 1. to connect 2. to tell or report
genuine [jen′ yoo in]	*adj.* real; true	**uncharted** [un chär′ təd]	*adj.* unexplored

Self-Tests

1 Circle the correct meaning of each vocabulary word.

1. **relate:**	keep back	tell
2. **ensure:**	make certain	doubt
3. **manipulative:**	freeing	controlling
4. **establish:**	form	destroy
5. **intimidated:**	scared	brave
6. **genuine:**	fake	real
7. **impress:**	interest	bore
8. **clarify:**	confuse	make clear
9. **uncharted:**	known	unexplored
10. **disclose:**	make public	hide

2 Complete the reading using the vocabulary words from the list below. Use each word once.

Vocabulary List

ensure	relate	disclose	uncharted	impress
established	genuine	clarify	intimidated	manipulative

"Hello, Denny? This is Ray. You won't believe it but last night I went to a seminar on flirting. Why? Because I want to date more and you know how it is sometimes—you see an attractive woman, and you don't know what to do or say. Well, sometimes I feel (1)_____. I don't suppose you know what that's like. Emma Mansfield told us what to do. She said she could (2)_____ we would meet people if we followed her advice. She said flirting isn't about being pushy or (3)_____. She really helped to (4)_____ some of the basics last night. She said you've got to remember three things. You should dress to (5)_____. Well, at least be clean and have your hair combed! Ha, ha! And try to get the person to look at you. What? Oh, there were women there—lots of them. People of all ages. There was one who was gorgeous. Did I talk to her? No, but I looked at her and she looked at me. You could say we (6)_____ eye contact. Why not? Well, we didn't learn what to say this time. Emma is going to (7)_____ that information in session two on how to talk to someone you like. Do you want to go with me next week? Come on, be a (8)_____ friend and go. Maybe we can practice together. Yeah, you help me (9)_____ to women, and I'll help you understand the man's points of view. Remember, our futures are (10)_____; we should have fun while we explore them. Is it a deal? Okay, Denise, see you later. Bye."

3 Put a T for True or F for False next to each statement according to the comments made by Emma Mansfield, the speaker on page 105.

_____ 1. Flirting is usually manipulative.

_____ 2. Emma ensured the crowd that they could meet new people while doing daily tasks.

_____ 3. According to Emma, you will be able to better navigate the uncharted world of love with her advice.

_____ 4. A lot of people at Emma's seminars feel too intimidated to flirt.

_____ 5. Establishing eye contact isn't important to Emma's rules of flirting.

_____ 6. The right kind of clothes can help you impress someone.

_____ 7. In Emma's seminar, she is going to disclose how to make more money.

_____ 8. Never show genuine interest; you may look pushy.

_____ 9. According to Emma, relating to someone is easier if you know her techniques.

_____ 10. Emma clarified that flirting was harmless.

4 Complete the sentences using the word list below. Use each word once.

Vocabulary List				
relate	genuine	ensure	uncharted	impressed
intimidated	clarify	manipulated	disclosed	established

1. Most of the planets in our solar system are _____.

2. I was _____ by the invitation to Nancy's party; it sounded like a very formal occasion.

3. I _____ myself by getting a perfect score on the test.

4. To _____ the time of the meeting, I called the secretary.

5. At a special meeting yesterday, the government _____ the contents of files that had been sealed for forty years.

6. I asked Grandpa to _____ the story about the time he got lost in a cave.

7. I _____ an exercise regimen to get back in shape.

8. The mother showed _____ love for her baby.

9. Margaret _____ the place cards at the dinner table so she was sitting next to Darrin.

10. To _____ success on the test, I studied all weekend and reread parts of the textbook.

Interactive Exercise

Create a simple drawing that illustrates two or three of the vocabulary words, or bring a picture from a magazine that could illustrate a few of the words and tape it to this page (or to a piece of paper). Underneath the picture, write a brief story using the words. Be prepared to share your picture and story in class.

Story:

_____

_____

_____

21 Word Parts III

Look for words with these **prefixes**, **roots**, and/or **suffixes** as you work through this book. You may have already seen some of them, and you will see others in later chapters. Learning basic word parts can help you figure out the meaning of unfamiliar words.

prefix: a word part added to the beginning of a word that changes the meaning of the root
root: a word's basic part with its essential meaning
suffix: a word part added to the end of a word; indicates the part of speech

WORD PART	MEANING	EXAMPLES AND DEFINITIONS
Prefixes		
con-, col-	together, with	*context:* a situation; involved with other elements *collaborative:* working together
re-	again, back	*review:* to look at something again *reflect:* to look back on
un-	not	*uncharted:* not charted or mapped *unwanted:* not wanted or desired
Roots		
-pas-, -pat-, -path-	feeling, disease	*sympathy:* a feeling of tenderness for someone's pain *psychopath:* a person with a disease of the mind
-que-, -qui-	to seek, to ask	*acquire:* to get something *request:* to seek permission
-spect-	look at	*inspection:* the act of looking into something *spectator:* someone who looks at something
-vis-, -vid-	see	*evident:* clearly seen *television:* a device for viewing images
Suffixes		
-ate, -ize (makes a verb)	to make	*anticipate:* to wait for; to look forward to *empathize:* to be understanding of
-ic, -al (makes an adjective)	relating to	*thematic:* relating to a theme or topic *musical:* relating to music
-ous, -ose (makes an adjective)	full of	*monotonous:* full of monotony; boring *morose:* full of sadness

Self-Tests

1 Read each definition and choose the appropriate word from the list below. Use each word once. The meaning of the word part is underlined to help you make the connection. Refer to the Word Part list if you need help.

Vocabulary List

passionate	evident	collaborate	inspect	relate
courageous	memorize	chronological	inquisitive	uninformed

1. to work <u>together</u> _____

2. to tell <u>again</u> _____

3. to <u>feel</u> strongly about _____

4. <u>full of</u> courage _____

5. <u>relating</u> to time order _____

6. to <u>make</u> part of memory _____

7. to <u>look</u> into something _____

8. plainly <u>seen</u> _____

9. <u>not</u> knowledgeable _____

10. <u>seeking</u> information _____

2 Finish the sentences with the meaning of each word part from the list below. Use each meaning once. The word part is underlined to help you make the connection.

Vocabulary List

look at	full of	disease	related to	with
to seek	not	to make	see	again

1. Because the in<u>vis</u>ible man was impossible to _____, he could overhear a lot of gossip about himself.

2. I am going to re<u>quest</u> tomorrow off from work. When I go _____ my boss's approval, I will tell him how important it is that I go skiing.

3. If you <u>re</u>peat a class, you have to take it _____.

4. A psycho<u>path</u> is a person with a mental _____.

5. Something <u>com</u>ical is _____ comedy.

Vocabulary List

look at	full of	disease	related to	with
to seek	not	to make	see	again

6. Because Tina is <u>con</u>genial, people like to work _____ her.

7. The wedding was a <u>joyous</u> occasion; it was _____ happiness.

8. The house was <u>un</u>usual because it did _____ have a front door.

9. I need to put on my <u>spect</u>acles to _____ the newspaper.

10. I fantas<u>ize</u> about being a famous pianist; _____ my dream come true I need to spend more time practicing.

3 Finish the story using the word parts below. Use each word part once. Your knowledge of word parts, as well as the context clues, will help you create the correct words. If you do not understand the meaning of a word you have made, check the dictionary for the definition or to see whether the word exists.

Vocabulary Parts

con	vis	al	ate	ous
qui	spect	un	re	path

THE SEARCH

Tony and Edie were looking for an inexpensive apartment to rent. Neither of them had jobs that provided much money. They in_____red about availability at one place and were told to come see it. The place was _____acular. The complex had a pool, a recreation area, and a laundry room. The bedrooms were so large they could easily accommod_____ four people. However, they were _____able to work it into their budgets. They had to be very economic_____.

They thought the chance of finding a two-bedroom apartment within their price range was impossible. Their friends sym_____ized with them, and said they would keep their eyes open. Then Lori called and said she knew how she could _____nect them with a good deal. She had just seen an ad on tele_____ion for apartments. The apartments were supposed to be affordable. They called the number and went to visit the place. The grounds and the apartment were wondr_____. They could not _____sist renting there. Their happiness was now complete.

4 Pick the best definition for each underlined word from the list below using your knowledge of word parts. Circle the word part in each of the underlined words.

a. to make a judgment
b. look into one's feelings
c. view
d. full of offense; disgraceful
e. overcome

f. have similar feelings
g. relating to drama
h. come together with force
i. to make new again
j. not good; regrettably

_____ 1. The vista of the lake from the path among the elms looked inviting.

_____ 2. My latest conquest was Mount Whitney. Now I have climbed every peak in the state.

_____ 3. After some introspection Gloria knew which job would be the best for her.

_____ 4. I should not always criticize my brother; sometimes I need to say something nice.

_____ 5. Unfortunately I forgot to bring spoons, so we will have to eat our ice cream with forks.

_____ 6. The student's dramatic presentation caused the class to weep.

_____ 7. I have to renew my library card; I haven't used it in four years.

_____ 8. My new roommate and I are compatible; we both like the same things.

_____ 9. If a space shuttle and a planet collide, there will be a huge mess.

_____ 10. Her low-cut dress was outrageous; it was not at all appropriate for a family gathering.

5 A good way to remember word parts is to pick one word that uses a word part and understand how that word part functions in the word. Then you can apply that meaning to other words that have the same word part. Use the words to help you match the word part to its meaning.

SET ONE

_____ 1. con-, col-: context, collaborative, congenial

_____ 2. –que-, -qui-: request, acquire, exquisite

_____ 3. –ic, -al: phonics, vital, philosophical

_____ 4. un-: unbridled, uncharted, uncertain

_____ 5. –spect-: inspect, aspect, spectator

a. look at
b. not
c. to seek
d. together, with
e. relating to

_____ 6. re-: repeat, retain, reflect   f. feeling, disease

_____ 7. –ate, -ize: passionate, prioritize, procrastinate   g. to make

_____ 8. –pas-, -pat-, -path-: passionate, sympathy, psychopath   h. full of

_____ 9. –vis-, -vid-: evident, visible, visionary   i. again, back

_____ 10. –ous, -ose: monotonous, villainous, morose   j. see

6 Use the dictionary to find a word you don't know that uses the word part. Write the meaning of the word part, the word, and the definition. If your dictionary has the etymology (history) of the word, see how the word part relates to the meaning, and write the etymology after the definition.

Word Part	Meaning	Word	Definition and Etymology
EXAMPLE:			
vid	see	videlicet	that is. Used to introduce examples or lists. Latin vidélicet, it is easy to see; vidére, to see + licet, it is permitted
1. *con-*			
2. *pat-*			
3. *re-*			

4. *spect-* _____

_____

_____

_____

5. *un-* _____

_____

_____

_____

22 Cleopatra (69–30 B.C.)

Are the Rumors True?*

Questions & Answers

Dear Cassandra,

I have heard **vague** rumors that the Egyptian queen Cleopatra VII is dead. Can that be possible? Please give me some details.

Aurora

Dear Reader,

The short answer to your **query** is "yes." But **further** information is surely necessary after all the space that has been **devoted** to Cleopatra's life in this column over the years. Cleopatra's life has been **hectic** beginning with a dispute with her brother Ptolemy that led to her exile in Syria. Julius Caesar, former ruler of the Roman Empire, fell in love with the young (21-year-old) Cleopatra while in Egypt following his defeat of Pompey. Caesar spent almost a year in Egypt helping Cleopatra regain her title. Their **bliss** was short lived as Cleopatra was forced to marry her eleven-year-old brother as Egyptian tradition demands; Caesar also had much to accomplish back in Rome. Caesar, as we know, was murdered on his return, ending the couple's short romance.

Mark Antony, ruler of the Eastern Roman Empire, met Cleopatra a few years after Caesar's death. Cleopatra's **ample** charms—beauty, intelligence, and wit—captured his heart also. Antony enjoyed a **lavish** life style in Egypt. Egyptian rulers are regarded as divine and are well taken care of. Antony reportedly carried a golden scepter and wore a crown. Now for the big problem—Antony was married to Octavian's

"When she heard that he was going to take her back to Rome as a slave, she killed herself."

sister. Octavian, ruler of the Western Roman Empire, became **livid** over Antony's betrayal of his sister. He persuaded the Roman Senate to declare war on Antony and Cleopatra. Antony's and Cleopatra's ships were defeated at the Battle of Actium. In the retreat, Antony was told that Cleopatra was dead, and he killed himself rather than live without her. (A reminder readers that true love can exist!) The news, however, was **inaccurate**. Cleopatra was very much alive, and supposedly trying to get Octavian to fall in love with her. She failed. When she heard that he was going to take her back to Rome as a slave, she killed herself. I have heard that she took poison or that she let an asp bite her. Either way, the life of one of the most fascinating women of our era has come to a sad end. This writer will surely miss her.

*Note: the letters are fictional.

Predicting

Circle the definition that best fits each vocabulary word. If you have difficulty, return to the reading on page 116, and underline any context clues you find. After you've made your predictions, check your answers against the Word List below. Place a checkmark in the boxes next to the words whose definitions you missed. These are the words you'll want to study closely.

Note: You may want to cover the Word List below with a piece of paper so you don't accidentally see the definitions as you do the Predicting exercise.

☐ 1. **vague** (line 3)
   a. definite
   b. uncertain
   c. strange

☐ 2. **query** (line 8)
   a. a question
   b. an answer
   c. a letter

☐ 3. **further** (line 9)
   a. less
   b. confusing
   c. more

☐ 4. **devoted** (line 10)
   a. ignored
   b. wondered about
   c. gave time or attention to

☐ 5. **hectic** (line 12)
   a. busy
   b. calm
   c. lovely

☐ 6. **bliss** (line 18)
   a. sadness
   b. absolute joy
   c. hide-away

☐ 7. **ample** (line 27)
   a. few
   b. colorful
   c. plentiful

☐ 8. **lavish** (line 29)
   a. extravagant
   b. long
   c. simple

☐ 9. **livid** (line 35)
   a. pleased
   b. amazed
   c. furious

☐ 10. **inaccurate** (line 43)
   a. mistaken
   b. positive
   c. funny

Word List

ample [am′ pəl]	*adj.*	plentiful; more than enough	**inaccurate** [in ak′ yər it]	*adj.* mistaken; incorrect
bliss [blis]	*n.*	absolute joy	**lavish** [lav′ ish]	*adj.* extravagant; abundant; generous *v.* to give or spend abundantly
devote [di vōt′]	*v.*	to promise; to give one's time or attention to	**livid** [liv′ id]	*adj.* 1. extremely angry; furious 2. of an abnormal color due to anger or illness
further [fûr′ THûr]	*adj.*	1. more; additional 2. more distant	**query** [kwēr′ ē]	*n.* a question
	v.	to promote; to favor		*v.* to question; to ask
hectic [hek′ tik]	*adj.*	busy and confused; feverish	**vague** [vāg]	*adj.* uncertain; not clearly expressed

Self-Tests

1 In Set One match each term with its synonym. In Set Two match each term with its antonym.

SYNONYMS			ANTONYMS		
SET ONE			**SET TWO**		
_____	1. lavish	a. incorrect	_____	6. ample	f. less
_____	2. inaccurate	b. ask	_____	7. hectic	g. sorrow
_____	3. devote	c. abundant	_____	8. bliss	h. insufficient
_____	4. livid	d. promise	_____	9. vague	i. relaxed
_____	5. query	e. furious	_____	10. further	j. sure

2 Answer each question with the appropriate vocabulary word. Use each word once.

SET ONE

1. What is "Do you like chocolate?" an example of? _____

2. What would directions that don't say whether to turn left or right at a T-intersection probably be called? _____

3. What would a person feel sipping an ice-cold drink on a hot day? _____

4. What would most people consider twelve pizzas for two people? _____

5. How would people likely describe an airport during the Thanksgiving holiday? _____

Vocabulary List

ample

bliss

vague

query

hectic

SET TWO

6. What would you be doing with your time if you volunteered three hours a week at a community center? _____

7. What would a check written yesterday, but dated 1995 be called? _____

8. What would your reaction likely be if you found your car bumper smashed? _____

9. What would Fern be doing for Darwin's career if she recommended him as an excellent candidate for the vice-president position at the company? _____

10. What would most people call a sports car as a present? _____

Vocabulary List

lavish

devoting

inaccurate

further

livid

3 Circle the word that correctly completes each sentence.

1. My mother was (hectic, livid) when I came home four hours late.

2. I wanted to (devote, further) more of my time to my schooling, so I am working six hours less this semester.

3. My (bliss, query) was destroyed when a water pipe broke, and I had to spend the day fixing it instead of relaxing on the porch with a good book.

4. My professor said there had been (vague, **ample**) time to get the project done, so he would not take late work.

5. I didn't understand why the hotel sent me their summer rates when my (**query**, bliss) had been about availability in the winter.

6. Because the weather reports had been (lavish, **inaccurate**) all week, I was uncertain about having my party outside on Saturday.

7. I had a (**vague**, further) feeling that I had forgotten something. When I got home to a wet floor, I realized I hadn't turned the bathtub off.

8. For my birthday my husband (**lavished**, devoted) gifts on me from opera tickets to a diamond necklace.

9. With two children under five, my sister finds most of her days to be (ample, **hectic**).

10. To get (**further**, livid) information on the company, I checked out their website.

4 The following are lines from fictitious letters between Cleopatra, Julius Caesar, and Mark Antony. Match each sentence to the word it best fits. Context clues are bolded to help you. Use each word once.

Vocabulary List

further	lavish	vague	inaccurate	devote
bliss	hectic	query	livid	ample

1. You've had **plenty** of time in Rome, Julius Caesar. Come back to Egypt now if you love me. _____

2. I am sorry Cleopatra, but life is **busy** in Rome. There are several political problems brewing that I must work to stop. _____

3. Julius Caesar, I am **furious** with you! Return now or we are through! _____

4. Cleopatra, I will return as soon as I can, and I promise **to give** all of my **time** to you. _____

5. Cleopatra, your **generous** charms have seduced me. I want to be yours. _____

6. Marc Antony, when I am with you my days are filled with **joy**. _____

7. Cleopatra, what **more** can I do to prove that I love you? _____

8. Marc Antony, I am **uncertain** about your feelings. Why have you married Octavius' sister when you say you love me? _____

9. Cleopatra, I have one **question**: do you really love me? _____

10. Antony, don't listen to stories that I am dead. They are a **mistake**. I am alive, and I miss you. _____

Interactive Exercise

List two examples for each question.

When might someone want to be vague?

1. _____

2. _____

When would one make a query?

1. _____

2. _____

When is further information important?

1. _____

2. _____

What is it easy to be inaccurate about?

1. _____

2. _____

What would you find at a lavish party?

1. _____

2. _____

What makes life hectic?

1. _____

2. _____

What brings bliss to your life?

1. _____

2. _____

What do you have ample of?

1. _____

2. _____

What makes you livid?

1. _____

2. _____

What activities are you devoted to?

1. _____

2. _____

23 Kublai Khan (1215–1294)

What the People Have to Say*

春秋 CHINA ⊛ TODAY 夏冬

What The People Have to Say.

Kublai Khan has been the Emperor of China for thirty years now (1260–90). What do people have
5 to say? How do they feel? To take a close **inspection** of his policies and actions *China Today* sent our staff out to ask people from officials of the court to peasants in the field their opinions. We asked the following question: What are your
10 impressions of Kublai Khan's reign?

Marco Polo (Venetian traveler and an official at the court since 1275):

Ruling a country is a **laborious** task, and Kublai Khan works extremely hard at it. I think that
15 overall he has done an excellent job. He has shown a tolerance for other religions. Buddhism is the most popular religion and what Kublai himself follows, but he has allowed Taoism and Roman Catholicism into China among other religions,
20 which is rare among leaders. His greatest achievement may be uniting such a large area through an advanced postal system. Messengers can surprisingly travel 250 miles a day. This development has improved communication within
25 the government and helped merchants. Though the Chinese have never been **jubilant** about their foreign ruler, Kublai Khan's interest in the arts has led to a period of great learning and culture. Kublai Khan is seventy-five years old now, and his
30 power seems more **tenuous** than it has at any time in the past thirty years, but I think he still has a few years left as a great emperor.

An anonymous Chinese lower official:

I am in a bit of a **quandary** of how to answer your question. Kublai Khan has improved our country 35 in some ways, but by getting rid of the civil service exams he has forced me and my Chinese **colleagues** into the lower ranks of government. He relies on the Mongol people and foreigners for the most important positions because he distrusts us. 40 It is difficult for us to be **supervised** by the Mongols and foreigners when we have a rich tradition of local governance. I feel that most Chinese do not embrace him or his rule.

Female Peasant: 45

Please do not print my name; I am afraid to **contradict** any official statements about what Kublai Khan has done for the people. To be honest, he has improved farming techniques and communication, but the people are growing **weary** 50 of the expensive wars against Japan. The attacks have failed, and led to greater taxes for us. I don't know what his **options** are for ending these attacks, but he should be trying to keep the common people happy, or he will find his Yuan 55 dynasty falling apart. You should have asked me ten years ago what I thought; the country was much better off then.

夏

*Note: the magazine interviews are fictitious.

Predicting

Circle the definition that best fits each vocabulary word. If you have difficulty, return to the reading on page 121, and underline any context clues you find. After you've made your predictions, check your answers against the Word List below. Place a checkmark in the boxes next to the words whose definitions you missed. These are the words you'll want to study closely.

NOTE: You may want to cover the Word List below with a piece of paper so you don't accidentally see the definitions as you do the Predicting exercise.

❑ 1. **inspection** (line 6)
a. a hiding place
b. a peek at
c. a close look at

❑ 2. **laborious** (line 13)
a. easy to do
b. requiring hard work
c. needing extra time

❑ 3. **jubilant** (line 26)
a. joyful
b. sad
c. angry

❑ 4. **tenuous** (line 30)
a. firm
b. scary
c. slight

❑ 5. **quandary** (line 34)
a. a passion
b. a confused state
c. a definite answer

❑ 6. **colleagues** (line 38)
a. enemies
b. strangers
c. co-workers

❑ 7. **supervised** (line 41)
a. controlled
b. carved
c. created

❑ 8. **contradict** (line 47)
a. to accept
b. to disagree with
c. to say loudly

❑ 9. **weary** (line 50)
a. rested
b. hungry
c. tired

❑ 10. **options** (line 53)
a. choices
b. plans
c. places

Word List

colleague
[käl′ ēg]
n. co-worker; associate; partner

contradict
[kän′ trə dikt′]
v. to disagree with; to deny; to be in conflict with

inspection
[in spek′ shən]
n. a close look at; official review

jubilant
[jōō′ bə lənt]
adj. joyful; thrilled

laborious
[lə bôr′ ē əs]
adj. 1. requiring hard work; difficult
2. hard-working; industrious

option
[op′ shən]
n. choosing; choice; alternative; the thing chosen

quandary
[kwon′ drē, -də rē]
n. a confused state; a difficulty

supervise
[sōō′ pər vīz′]
v. to oversee; to conduct; to control the performance of work or workers

tenuous
[ten′ yōō əs]
adj. slight; weak; thin

weary
[wēr′ ē]
adj. tired; exhausted
v. to tire; to grow tired

Self-Tests

1 Circle the correct meaning of each vocabulary word.

1.	**contradict:**	to agree	to deny
2.	**options:**	choices	limitations
3.	**tenuous:**	slight	firm
4.	**colleague:**	enemy	associate
5.	**inspection:**	glance	examination
6.	**weary:**	tired	energetic
7.	**laborious:**	lazy	hard-working
8.	**supervise:**	conduct	follow
9.	**quandary:**	certain	confused
10.	**jubilant:**	dejected	joyful

2 Finish the sentences using the vocabulary words. Use each word once.

Vocabulary List

option

colleagues

inspection

laborious

quandary

weary

jubilant

contradict

tenuous

supervise

1. I was in a _____ about whether to go to my high school reunion or a friend's wedding. Luckily, for me, the wedding was postponed.

2. I will let you drive my car as long as I can _____. You need to listen to what I tell you.

3. My _____ and I had a productive meeting. We settled several issues that had been hurting the work environment.

4. Relaxing isn't a(n) _____ when my grandmother comes to visit; she likes to keep busy all day.

5. The _____ revealed that the heads of the company had been hiding money in a secret account for years.

6. I hate to _____ the instructor, but she said the test would be in two days, which is a Sunday, and we don't have class on Sundays.

7. The king's control of the country was _____. The people were rebelling, and only the promise of greater freedom could stop them.

8. The crowd was _____ until the announcer said there might be a penalty, and the goal wouldn't count.

9. The long speech was beginning to bore the _____ audience.

10. Doing a research paper seemed _____ to me until I looked it as a big puzzle.

3 Put a T for true or F for false next to each statement.

_____ 1. An airplane must go through an inspection before it is allowed to fly.

_____ 2. One should try to get along with one's colleagues.

_____ 3. Deciding what to major in can be a quandary for some people.

_____ 4. Most people like to be contradicted all the time.

_____ 5. People who go crazy usually have a tenuous hold on reality.

_____ 6. A team would be jubilant about their season if they lost all their games.

_____ 7. Getting a good night's sleep usually makes people feel weary.

_____ 8. Most people find relaxing in a lounge chair a laborious task.

_____ 9. If a coat only comes in black, one has several options as to color.

_____ 10. Children should be supervised when they play in a swimming pool.

4 Use the vocabulary words to complete the following analogies. For instructions on how to complete analogies, see the Analogies Appendix on page 143.

Vocabulary List

inspection	tenuous	weary	option	quandary
supervise	laborious	jubilant	contradict	colleague

1. mowing the neighbor's lawn : kindness :: what to wear on a big date : _____

2. run : race :: _____ : workers

3. laugh : a joke :: _____ : a long drive

4. expensive : cheap :: support : _____

5. a speeding ticket : mad :: an "A" on a paper : _____

6. empty : blank :: slight : _____

7. math : subject :: the blue or the red : _____

8. ask : query :: _____ : partner

9. rehearsal : play :: _____ : restaurant

10. separate : unite :: _____ : easy

Interactive Exercise

Answer the following questions.

1. How did you deal with a quandary in your life?

   _____

2. What task do you consider laborious?

   _____

3. When might you need to contradict someone?

   _____

4. What makes you weary?

   _____

5. What is something one should never say to a colleague? Why?

   _____

6. What are two items or places that should have at least a yearly inspection?

   _____

7. What kind of activity would you like to supervise?

   _____

8. Where would you find jubilant people?

   _____

9. What do you have a tenuous understanding of?

   _____

10. What is a recent option you have been faced with? Did you make the right choice?

   _____

Simon Bolivar
(1783–1830)

From the Liberator's Journal*

November 1815

I am not **invincible**. I have had to flee here to Jamaica since my countrymen who are still loyal to
Spain have taken back Caracas. The losses of the last five years have been an **affront** to my pride,
but I have the **resolve** to continue. I will help to **secure** the freedom of South America. I want to
5   establish a balance of powers based on the British model of government. My voice will be heard!

July 1825

My **noble** efforts have been rewarded. I have
helped to free the upper section of Peru, and it has
been renamed Bolivia in my honor. The wars are
10   coming to an end. I can now focus on being the
president of Colombia. For the last six years the
vice-president has had to keep the country in
order. During the **interim**, I have been busy as
commander-in-chief of the military, but now I am
15   ready to take over my political responsibilities. I
hope there is **adequate** time to get all I want
done. My dear wife—I miss you Maria Teresa.
Why did you have to die so young? I will never
marry again. What would you think of the name
20   the people have given me, El Libertador?

May 1830

The last years have not been good. **Aside** from my failed attempt to create a union among the
countries formerly controlled by Spain, I could not satisfy the different sides in Colombia, and I had
to become a dictator. The assassination attempt in 1828 terrified me! Finally, resignation was my
25   only choice, and tomorrow I head into exile again. I am sick with tuberculosis and may not live
much longer, but I do not want to be **morose**. I know that I helped to free my homeland, and if a
monument is ever created to honor me, I hope the people will **inscribe** on it, "A man who fought
for freedom; a man who wanted peace."

*Note: the journal entries are fictitious.

Predicting

Circle the definition that best fits each vocabulary word. If you have difficulty, return to the reading on page 126, and underline any context clues you find. After you've made your predictions, check your answers against the Word List below. Place a checkmark in the boxes next to the words whose definitions you missed. These are the words you'll want to study closely.

NOTE: You may want to cover the Word List below with a piece of paper so you don't accidentally see the definitions as you do the Predicting exercise.

❑ 1. **invincible** (line 2)
  a. lazy
  b. fragile
  c. undefeatable

❑ 2. **affront** (line 3)
  a. insult
  b. kindness
  c. reminder

❑ 3. **resolve** (line 4)
  a. weakness
  b. determination
  c. a list

❑ 4. **secure** (line 4)
  a. to succeed in getting
  b. to think about
  c. to fail

❑ 5. **noble** (line 7)
  a. selfish
  b. admirable
  c. careful

❑ 6. **interim** (line 13)
  a. time to go
  b. time wasted
  c. time in between

❑ 7. **adequate** (line 16)
  a. too much
  b. enough
  c. too little

❑ 8. **aside** (line 22)
  a. apart
  b. together
  c. close

❑ 9. **morose** (line 26)
  a. happy
  b. miserable
  c. calm

❑ 10. **inscribe** (line 27)
  a. to dance
  b. to build
  c. to write on

Word List

adequate
[ad' i kwit]
adj. sufficient; satisfactory; enough

affront
[ə frunt']
n. an insult
v. to insult; to confront

aside
[ə sīd']
adv. to or on one side; away; apart
n. words spoken confidentially by an actor to the audience

inscribe
[in skrīb']
v. to write or carve on a surface or page

interim
[in' tər əm]
n. time in between
adj. temporary

invincible
[in vin' sə bəl]
adj. unconquerable; undefeatable; powerful

morose
[mə rōs']
adj. gloomy; miserable; depressed

noble
[nō' bəl]
adj. 1. admirable; distinguished; of excellent character
  2. well-born; aristocratic
n. a nobleman or noblewoman

resolve
[ri zolv']
n. determination; a firm decision or plan
v. 1. to make up one's mind; to decide firmly
  2. to solve or settle, such as an argument

secure
[sə kyoor']
v. 1. to succeed in getting
  2. to make safe
adj. safe; reliable

Self-Tests

Put a T for true or F for false next to each statement.

_____ 1. Waving at someone and saying "Hi" is usually considered an affront.

_____ 2. Serving as president of an organization until a permanent president can be found is an example of an interim position.

_____ 3. One might inscribe a message on an engagement ring.

_____ 4. Locking your house can help to make it secure.

_____ 5. A week of rain can make some people morose.

_____ 6. A banana is an adequate lunch for most people.

_____ 7. Unsure about what color to paint a room shows resolve.

_____ 8. Cheating on a test would be a noble action.

_____ 9. If you were to step aside, you would move away from your current spot.

_____ 10. Losing ten games in a row would be the record for an invincible team.

2 Complete the sentences by using the word list below. Use each word once.

Vocabulary List				
inscribed	aside	secure	invincible	resolved
noble	affront	interim	morose	adequate

1. We have an _____ supply of food for the party.

2. While you look at shoes, I will spend the _____ trying on clothes.

3. If I were Superman (except for Kryptonite), I would be _____.

4. Chester seems _____; he is always wearing a frown.

5. I was able to _____ tickets to the sold-out concert.

6. I can't believe the _____. That man just walked up to me and called me ugly.

7. I _____ a note in the book I gave my mother.

8. It was _____ of Martin to help establish peace in the neighborhood again after he was falsely accused of the lawn mower incident.

9. The actor whispered an _____ to the audience.

10. The parties _____ the contract dispute after three months of arguing.

In Set One match each term with its synonym. In Set Two match each term with its antonym.

SYNONYMS

SET ONE

_____ 1. adequate   a. safe

_____ 2. aside   b. enough

_____ 3. inscribe   c. apart

_____ 4. secure   d. well-born

_____ 5. noble   e. carve

ANTONYMS

SET TWO

_____ 6. interim   f. cheerful

_____ 7. invincible   g. compliment

_____ 8. resolve   h. permanent

_____ 9. morose   i. hesitate

_____ 10. affront   j. weak

4 Finish the reading using the vocabulary words. Use each word once.

Vocabulary List				
noble	interim	adequate	inscribed	morose
aside	secure	affront	resolve	invincible

When I was a child, an old man told me a story about his fighting with Simon Bolivar. He said that one time Bolivar had to leave his troops for a month to take care of business in Columbia. During the (1)_____ the men got restless. When he returned he found them (2)_____: they had lost heart in their campaign. Bolivar had to restore their (3)_____. He addressed the troops: "The Spaniards actions are a(n) (4)_____ to our pride. All men have a right to freedom. Haven't I provided you all with (5)_____ food and supplies? (6)_____ from a few lonely nights what have you really suffered? Remember our mission is a(n) (7)_____ one. We are in the right! Are you ready to (8)_____ your freedom?" The men yelled "Si!" They now felt (9)_____. Before they left the next morning, the old man (10)_____ the words, "Gracias, Simon" on a rock nearby. I always wanted to find that rock.

Interactive Exercise

Write three journal entries about an experience or event that was important to you. Use at least seven of the vocabulary words in your entries.

Date: _____

_____

_____

_____

_____

_____

Date: _____

_____

_____

_____

_____

_____

Date: _____

_____

_____

_____

_____

_____

25 Victoria Woodhull
(1838–1927)

The First Female Candidate for President*

LETTERS TO THE EDITOR

November 1872

Dear Editor,

I was sorry to read your article that trumpeted the failure of Victoria Woodhull's presidential run. That Woodhull had to end her **historic** bid for president by spending election night in jail is a crime. Woodhull was the first female candidate for president of the United States, and I hope not the last. The **circumstances** surrounding her campaign were filled with unusual troubles. The **genesis** of Mrs. Woodhull's running for the highest office in this country may have come from her attendance at the 1869 National Female Suffrage Convention, which I also attended. Woodhull has been a strong promoter of equality for women. Some of Woodhull's ideas have been **offensive** to people such as her support of free love. Her **claim** that the popular Reverend Beecher was unfaithful to his wife has also made several members of the public **irate**. The assertions that have appeared in her paper, *Woodhull and Clafin's Weekly*, on Beecher's affair with his best friend's wife are in part what led to her being arrested for sending obscene literature through the mail. A ridiculous charge! The Beecher family has been against Woodhull's campaign from the beginning.

I know Mrs. Woodhull realized that running for president was a difficult task, and she understood that to win she needed money and public support, both of which she had at one time. As the first female stockbroker, Woodhull was not **naïve** about financial matters. However, I am sure she did not sense how cruel some people would be and how they would set out to ruin her campaign and her life. I hope Woodhull's disaster is not the **harbinger** of more ill-will for women trying to enter politics. Women will no longer remain **spectators** in politics; we are ready to be participants. The public needs to understand that women will not **waver**. We are moving forward. Women will get the right to vote, and a woman will be president of the United States some day.

With hope for the future,

Elizabeth Cady Stanton

*Note: the letter is fictitious.

Predicting

Circle the definition that best fits each vocabulary word. If you have difficulty, return to the reading on page 131, and underline any context clues you find. After you've made your predictions, check your answers against the Word List below. Place a checkmark in the boxes next to the words whose definitions you missed. These are the words you'll want to study closely.

NOTE: You may want to cover the Word List below with a piece of paper so you don't accidentally see the definitions as you do the Predicting exercise.

❑ 1. **historic** (line 10)
   a. unimportant
   b. famous in history
   c. old

❑ 2. **circumstances** (line 14)
   a. conditions around an event
   b. the beginning of a campaign
   c. problems

❑ 3. **genesis** (line 16)
   a. end
   b. intelligence
   c. beginning

❑ 4. **offensive** (line 23)
   a. insulting
   b. appealing
   c. inviting

❑ 5. **claim** (line 24)
   a. a lie
   b. a declaration
   c. a story

❑ 6. **irate** (line 27)
   a. pleased
   b. tired
   c. angry

❑ 7. **naïve** (line 40)
   a. ignorant
   b. knowledgeable
   c. careless

❑ 8. **harbinger** (line 45)
   a. a thing that brings bad news
   b. a person who invests in stocks
   c. a person or thing that announces the approach of another

❑ 9. **spectators** (line 47)
   a. women who run for office
   b. people who watch
   c. people who vote

❑ 10. **waver** (line 49)
   a. to hide
   b. to confirm
   c. to hesitate

Word List

circumstance [sûr′ kəm stans′]	*n.* 1. a fact or condition around an event (often plural) 2. (plural) one's financial condition	**historic** [his tôr′ ik]	*adj.* famous or important in history; notable
		irate [ī rāt′]	*adj.* angry; enraged; furious
claim [klām]	*n.* 1. a declaration or assertion 2. a demand or request *v.* 1. to declare; to assert 2. to demand as one's due	**naïve** [nä ēv′]	*adj.* ignorant; innocent; simple
		offensive [ô fen′ siv, ə fen′ siv]	*adj.* 1. insulting; disgusting 2. aggressive; attacking *n.* aggressive action or attitude
genesis [jen′ ə sis]	*n.* origin; beginning	**spectator** [spek′ tāt′ ər]	*n.* a person who watches
harbinger [här′ bin jər]	*n.* a person or thing that announces the approach of another; forerunner	**waver** [wā′ vər]	*v.* 1. to be unsure; to hesitate 2. to swing or move back and forth 3. to shake, used of a sound

Self-Tests

1 Write the word from the list below next to its definition.

Vocabulary List

claim	harbinger	naïve	spectator	waver
genesis	historic	irate	offensive	circumstances

1. a person who watches _____

2. origin; beginning _____

3. one's financial condition _____

4. famous or important in history _____

5. to move back and forth _____

6. ignorant _____

7. furious _____

8. a demand or request _____

9. an aggressive action or attitude _____

10. a person or thing that announces the approach of another _____

2 In each group circle the word that does not have a connection to the other three words.

1. claim	declare	assert	deny
2. harbinger	forerunner	harvest	approach
3. irate	calm	angry	enraged
4. simple	experienced	innocent	naïve
5. participant	viewer	spectator	observer
6. condition	circumstance	fact	isolation
7. offensive	pleasant	insulting	aggressive
8. genesis	origin	result	start
9. swing	waver	unsure	positive
10. historic	notable	average	famous

3 Match each sentence to the word it illustrates. Context clues are underlined to help you. Look for synonyms, antonyms, examples, or general meaning of a sentence. Use each word once.

SET ONE

Vocabulary List

irate	offensive	historic	spectator	naïve

1. "What an amazing throw! I'm so glad I came to see the game." _____

2. "I thought he was polite, but he came up to me and said, "Your haircut is horrible." _____

3. "I've never done this before." _____

4. "I can't believe they made a mistake on my credit card bill again!" _____

5. "This house was built in 1854. It is the oldest structure in town." _____

SET TWO

Vocabulary List

waver	claim	genesis	harbinger	circumstances

6. "My assertion is that I returned the book despite what the library insists." _____

7. "The accident happened on a snowy morning on a deserted road." _____

8. "I hate to hesitate, but now that it is raining I'm not sure I want to go." _____

9. "When the club began, it only had five people, and now it has two hundred." _____

10. "The birds are returning; spring can't be far behind." _____

4 Finish the headlines. Use each word once.

Vocabulary List

offensive	genesis	spectator	naïve	harbinger
claims	irate	waver	historic	circumstances

1. _____ House Up for Sale—Owner Says "George Washington Slept Here!"

2. Family _____ Force Candidate to Withdraw from Governor's Race

3. _____ of County's Financial Problems Stem from Five-Year-Old Decision

4. New Barbeque Restaurant's Odors Found _____ by Next Door Businesses

5. Presidential Candidate _____ Conspiracy Against Her Campaign

6. *Townspeople _____ Over Increased Taxes*

7. Several _____ People Fooled by Phone Fraud

8. *Is Early Snowfall a _____ of a Long Winter?*

9. *Conservation Group Won't _____ : Historic Barn Must Be Saved*

10. _____ Falls from Tree While Watching Presidents' Day Parade

Interactive Exercise

Pretend you are a journalist covering Woodhull's presidential campaign. Using six of the vocabulary words, write questions you want to ask at her next press conference. You don't need to know the answers to the questions. For example: What would you do, Mrs. Woodhull, if you were president and an irate citizen started yelling at you while you were addressing a meeting?

1. _____

2. _____

3. _____

4. _____

5. _____

6. _____

26 Review

Focus on Chapters 18–25

1. _____

2. _____

3. _____

4. _____

5. _____

6. _____

7. _____

8. _____

9. _____

10. _____

11. _____

12. _____

The following activities give you a chance to interact some more with the vocabulary words you've been learning. By looking at art, acting, writing, taking tests, and doing a crossword puzzle, you will see which words you know well and which you still need to work with.

Art

Match each picture on page 136 with one of the following vocabulary words. Use each word once.

Vocabulary List

confidential	tenderness	livid	tenuous
noble	spectator	intimidate	hectic
historic	lament	weary	inscribe

Collaborative Activity: Drama

Charades: You will be given one of the following words to act out in class. Think about how this word can be demonstrated without speaking. The other people in class will try to guess what word you are showing.

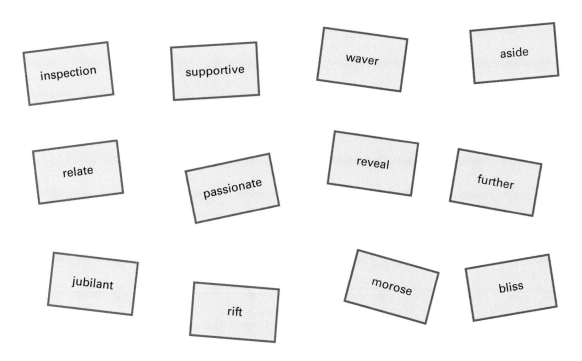

inspection

supportive

waver

aside

relate

passionate

reveal

further

jubilant

rift

morose

bliss

Writing

Answer the following questions to further test your understanding of the vocabulary words.

1. Whom would you share an intimate secret with? Why? _____

   _____

2. When were you able to empathize with a friend? _____

   _____

3. What is one of the most offensive smells to you?

   _____

4. When were you willing to compromise? _____

   _____

5. What are two events that it would be good to establish deadlines for?

   _____

   _____

6. What can someone do to become less gullible? _____

   _____

7. What are two areas that are still uncharted in this world?

   _____   _____

8. What topic do you have a genuine interest in?

   _____

9. How many hours of sleep do you consider adequate for you?

   _____

10. Where would you likely see someone supervising?

    _____

Self-Tests

I Finish the story using the vocabulary words below. Use each word once.

THE PARTY

I thought that throwing a party to show my appreciation to all my friends for their support when I was ill would be easy: I was wrong. My preliminary estimate that it would cost about $100 was way too low. I spent $105 on decorations, plates, and games alone. I then (1)_____ to make a firm budget. To (2)_____ a successful party, I would need to plan carefully.

The night of the party arrived, and I (3)_____ how nice my house looked. I was encouraged about the success of the party when the first guests complimented me on the good food and beautiful decorations. Then something remarkable happened, and the mood of the party began to change as more people came. My awareness of the problem was slow, but I came to feel that there was tension in the room. I couldn't figure out what (4)_____ was causing people to start whispering in small groups. To verify that something was going on, I asked my best friend for her opinion. She told me that someone had started a (5)_____ story about me. I was (6)_____ that someone would say mean things about me. How could one of my friends do that? I cautiously tried to find the identity of the person who was spreading the gossip. His or her cover, however, was (7)_____.

Finally, I stood up on a chair and said, "For the benefit of everyone here, I want to announce that the story circulating about me is (8)_____. Someone has made a huge mistake about my illness. The support of real friends has empowered me to make this statement. I had (9)_____ that everyone here was a friend. (10)_____, I was wrong. To those people who really do care about me, thank you for coming to my party." As the clapping began, I heard the front door open and shut. I never figured out who left, but I enjoyed the rest of the evening with some great friends.

Vocabulary List

admired

affronted

apparently

assumed

circumstance

ensure

inaccurate

invincible

malicious

resolved

2 Pick the word that best completes the sentence.

1. Karl was _____ that the store was closed; he really wanted a bag of potato chips.

   a. intimate   b. irate   c. intimidated   d. inaccurate

2. Alicia _____ her free time to helping children learn to read.

   a. establishes   b. laments   c. devotes   d. reveals

3. Dan showed his _____ when he bought low and sold high in the stock market.

   a. sympathy   b. shrewdness   c. claim   d. inspection

4. Chet _____ ever taking the trip; it was one disaster after another.

   a. admired   b. lamented   c. contradicted   d. neglected

5. I was shocked when Elizabeth _____ her secret that she was from outer space.

   a. supervised   b. compromised   c. disclosed   d. wavered

6. I gave myself _____ time to drive to my grandmother's house, but I was still late because of a huge accident on the freeway that delayed me for three hours.

   a. ample   b. confidential   c. lavish   d. malicious

7. My _____ and I are busy preparing a presentation for a conference next week.

   a. spectator   b. bliss   c. rift   d. colleague

8. I worked hard to _____ front row seats at the tennis tournament; they were not easy to get.

   a. relate   b. secure   c. reveal   d. clarify

9. My professor thought my responses on the quiz were _____; she said I needed more details.

   a. vague   b. jubilant   c. passionate   d. weary

10. I considered all my _____ before I bought my car; I am happy with my choice.

   a. impressions   b. colleagues   c. asides   d. options

Crossword Puzzle

Across

4. to display
9. "I'm confused about who to talk to."
10. to make public
12. to interest
13. controlling
15. to overlook
16. "You are so wrong!"
17. beginning
18. an extreme interest in
19. the kind of card one would send to a recent widow

Down

1. to ask
2. extravagant; abundant
3. I need to _____ my points, so people will understand me
5. hard-working
6. to tell or report
7. simple; innocent
8. swimsuits for sale are a _____ of summer
11. temporary
14. this can be good or bad
16. a declaration or assertion

Use the following words to complete the crossword puzzle. Use each word once.

Vocabulary List

advice

claim

clarify

contradict

disclose

fascination

genesis

harbinger

impress

interim

laborious

lavish

manipulative

naïve

neglect

quandary

query

relate

reveal

sympathy

Analogies Appendix

An **analogy** shows a relationship between words. Working with analogies helps one to see connections between items, which is a crucial critical thinking skill. Analogies are written as follows: big : large :: fast : quick. The colon (:) means *is to*. The analogy reads big *is to* large as fast *is to* quick. To complete analogies simply find a relationship between the first pair of words and then look for a similar relationship in another set of words. In the example above *big* and *large* are synonyms and so are *fast* and *quick*.

Common relationships used in analogies are synonyms, antonyms, examples, part to a whole, grammatical structure, cause and effect, sequences, and an object to a user or to its use.

Analogies in this book come in matching and fill-in-the-blank forms. Try the following analogies for practice.

Matching

1. old : young ::   _____
2. clip coupons :: go shopping   _____
3. peel : banana ::   _____
4. no rain : drought ::   _____

a. preface : book
b. put on shoes : take a walk
c. low wages : strike
d. rested : tired

Fill-in-the-Blank

writer	passion	abduct	sadly

5. frozen : chilled :: kidnap : _____

6. interrupting : rude :: embracing : _____

7. slow : slowly :: sad : _____

8. baton : conductor :: computer : _____

Answers

1. d   [antonyms]
2. b   [sequence]
3. a   [part to a whole]
4. c   [cause and effect]
5. abduct   [synonyms]
6. passion   [an example]
7. sadly   [grammatical structure]
8. writer   [object to user]

Limited Answer Key

CHAPTER 1   Vocabulary Basics
Predicting

1. c	3. b	5. a	7. b	9. c
2. b	4. a	6. c	8. c	10. a

CHAPTER 2   College Life
Predicting

1. c	3. c	5. a	7. a	9. a
2. c	4. a	6. c	8. c	10. a

CHAPTER 3   Time Management
Predicting

1. c	3. b	5. c	7. b	9. b
2. a	4. b	6. a	8. b	10. a

CHAPTER 5   Collecting
Predicting

1. b	3. b	5. a	7. b	9. c
2. a	4. c	6. c	8. a	10. c

CHAPTER 6   Travel
Predicting

1. b	3. c	5. a	7. a	9. b
2. a	4. b	6. c	8. c	10. a

CHAPTER 7   Computers
Predicting

1. a	3. c	5. a	7. a	9. b
2. a	4. b	6. c	8. c	10. c

CHAPTER 9   Art
Predicting

1. b	3. c	5. b	7. a	9. c
2. a	4. c	6. a	8. b	10. b

CHAPTER 10   Music
Predicting

1. b	3. b	5. a	7. b	9. c
2. a	4. b	6. a	8. c	10. c

CHAPTER 11   Books
Predicting

1. b	3. a	5. b	7. c	9. a
2. b	4. b	6. c	8. a	10. c

CHAPTER 12   Movies
Predicting

1. b	3. b	5. a	7. a	9. c
2. c	4. a	6. a	8. b	10. c

CHAPTER 14 Fitness
Predicting

1. a	3. a	5. c	7. c	9. b
2. a	4. b	6. b	8. b	10. a

CHAPTER 15 Personal Finance
Predicting

1. a	3. b	5. a	7. a	9. b
2. c	4. b	6. a	8. a	10. a

CHAPTER 16 The World
Predicting

1. c	3. b	5. b	7. c	9. b
2. a	4. a	6. a	8. b	10. a

CHAPTER 18 Personalities
Predicting

1. b	3. c	5. b	7. a	9. c
2. c	4. c	6. a	8. b	10. b

CHAPTER 19 Friendship
Predicting

1. b	3. a	5. c	7. a	9. b
2. b	4. b	6. b	8. c	10. a

CHAPTER 20 Romance
Predicting

1. a	3. a	5. a	7. a	9. a
2. b	4. c	6. c	8. b	10. b

CHAPTER 22 Cleopatra
Predicting

1. b	3. c	5. a	7. c	9. c
2. a	4. c	6. b	8. a	10. a

CHAPTER 23 Kublai Khan
Predicting

1. c	3. a	5. b	7. a	9. c
2. b	4. c	6. c	8. b	10. a

CHAPTER 24 Simon Bolivar
Predicting

1. c	3. b	5. b	7. b	9. b
2. a	4. a	6. c	8. a	10. c

CHAPTER 25 Victoria Woodhull
Predicting

1. b	3. c	5. b	7. a	9. b
2. a	4. a	6. c	8. c	10. c

Create Your Own Flash Cards

Using flash cards can be an immensely helpful way to study vocabulary words. The process of making the flash cards will aid you in remembering the meanings of the words. Index cards work well as flash cards. Put the word and the pronunciation on the front of the card. Elements you may want to include on the back of the cards will vary according to the word and your preferred learning style. Consider the ideas below and find what works best for you.

1. **The part of speech:** Write an abbreviation for the part of speech, such as n. for noun or v. for verb. This addition will help when you are writing sentences.
2. **A simple definition:** Use the definitions in the book or modify them to something that has meaning for you. Use a definition you can remember.
3. **A sentence:** Make up your own sentence that correctly uses the word. Try to use a context clue to help you remember the word. It might help to put yourself or friends in the sentences to personalize your use of the word. If you really like a sentence from the book, you can use that too.
4. **A drawing:** If you are a visual learner, try drawing the word. Some words especially lend themselves to this method. Your drawing doesn't have to be fancy; it should just help you remember the meaning of the word.
5. **A mnemonic (ni mon' ik) device:** These are methods to help your memory. They can be rhymes, formulas, or clues. For example: Station*e*ry with an *e* is the kind that goes in an *e*nvelope. Make up any connections you can between the word and its meaning.
6. **Highlight word parts:** Circle one or more word parts (prefixes, roots, or suffixes) that appear in the word and write the meaning(s) next to the word part: for example, disorganized. See the Word Parts chapters in the text for more on word parts.   → not

Whatever you do, make the cards personally meaningful. Find the techniques that work for you and use them in creating your cards. Then make the time to study the cards. Carry them with you and study any chance you get. Also, find someone who will be tough in quizzing you with the cards. Have the person hold up a card, and you give the meaning and use the word in a sentence. Don't quit until you are confident that you know what each word means. You may use the following pages of flash card templates to get you started.

Sample card

Front

audible

[ô də bəl]

Back

adj. loud enough to hear

Even though she was whispering, Liz's comments were audible across the room.

Word List